THE MISSING PIECE

How Successful Companies
Develop High-Performance Cultures

DEAN HALLETT

Copyright © 2021
Dean Hallett

Performance Publishing Group
McKinney, TX

All Worldwide Rights Reserved.

All rights reserved. No part of this publication may be reproduced, stored in a retrieval system or transmitted, in any form or by any means, electronic, mechanical, recorded, photocopied, or otherwise, without the prior written permission of the copyright owner, except by a reviewer who may quote brief passages in a review.

ISBN: 978-1-956914-59-7 (paperback)
978-1-956914-22-1 (hardcover)

Testimonials

"*The Missing Piece is a powerful roadmap for shifting your organization into high performance!*"

Jeffery Kendall
Chairman and CEO
Nymbus, Inc.

"*The Accelerated Leadership Program (ALP) was the most valuable program I participated in during my 12-year tenure at Fox. Despite already having an MBA and a decade of executive experience, the program provided a more personal and reflective approach that helped me leverage my strengths, develop heightened self-awareness, and build the courage to be a results-producing leader under all types of business circumstances.*"

Cameron Dillavou
Global Head of Go-To-Market Strategy
Amazon Prime Video

"*Dean is an accomplished executive who has compiled a truly successful track record in both his business and personal life. As an executive coach, he brings a unique blend of experience, thought leadership and motivational tactics. He has proven to be a true mentor who has challenged me, supported me and inspired me to think differently.*"

Mike Terzian
President and CEO
Foothill Credit Union

"The ALP program brought together smart, motivated people and helped them develop the tools to tackle real business challenges. The executives grew immeasurably in the program and the company benefited enormously from their contributions."

Ted Russell
Senior Executive/Attorney
Media Entertainment Industry

"The ALP program gave me the confidence I needed to become a proactive decision-maker, and taught me to trust my instincts in the process."

Robin Geisen
Motion Picture Marketing Executive
Creative Artists Agency

"The ALP program pushed me out of my comfort zone, which allowed me to be a more effective leader, not just an individual performer, and provided me with the tools for sustained growth and development as an executive."

Kobie Conner
Director, Business Legal Affairs
Netflix Original Independent Films

"The ALP program helped me to better understand my inherent strengths as a leader and develop effective soft skills, while also gaining a stronger understanding of how I could contribute to the company's overall goals. It ultimately reinforced my loyalty to the company, as I appreciated the investment they made in me."

Adriana Trautman
VP International Strategy
Paramount Pictures

TESTIMONIALS

"Continued improvement and development are essential for a successful career. Even the most acclaimed actors, athletes, and executives use coaches and advisors. Hallett Leadership offers effective methods and practices relevant for today's business leaders. I highly recommend Dean as a professional resource to stay on top of your game!"

Ron Frierson
Director of Economic Policy
Office of the Mayor, Los Angeles

"The ALP teams' recommendations pushed executives to think differently about critical business issues and often resulted in the launch of a new initiative or an organizational change. I would highly recommend this program because it not only developed the talent within the ALP, but it also fostered an overall culture of collaboration and innovation."

Beth Kearns
Former Executive Vice President
Operations Strategy, 20th Century Fox

"ALP is one of the most impactful, innovative leadership programs I've seen. Employees that go through the program contribute at a more strategic level, have a greater perspective on contribution across the enterprise, and quite simply are just more confident leaders."

Dave Shaw
Executive Leadership Coach
Dave Shaw and Associates

"The Accelerated Leadership Program gave me the tools to grow as a leader, enhance my presentation skills, and develop my interpersonal/management skills, ultimately creating much stronger relationships with my colleagues."

Jessica Wichard
Senior Director, Retail Development
Jazwares, LLC

"Participating in the Accelerated Leadership Program was deeply empowering for me as a person, as well as a professional. It gave me the strength to risk and grow as a practitioner, a team member, and an entrepreneur."

Marina Kösten
Head of Research & Strategy
StoryFit

"Dean's years of real-world executive experience at The Walt Disney Company and Fox Studios was a real differentiating factor as an executive coach. His ability to pull from his own efforts, combined with pragmatic, field-tested approaches and solutions, allowed me to really raise my leadership capabilities."

Chris Parker
President and CEO
Northeast Credit Union

"Dean's innovative, creative, and hands-on approach allows for a fun and collaborative experience where participants are challenged to push conventional wisdom, think outside the box, and become change drivers in their organizations."

Novena Catalla-Kam
Global Content Operations Strategy Leader
Amazon Prime Video

Dedication

This book is dedicated to my family: my wife Kelli,
my wonderful partner for the past 38 years,
and our children, Drew and Makenzie,
for always believing in me.

Table of Contents

Testimonials iii

Dedication vii

Acknowledgments xi

Foreword xiii

Introduction 1

Chapter 1: The Importance of People 13

Chapter 2: Authentic Leadership 27

Chapter 3: Alignment 47

Chapter 4: Building the Best Teams 67

Chapter 5: An Open Culture and the Value of Feedback 91

Chapter 6: Collaboration and Empowerment 113

Chapter 7: Creativity and Innovation 133

Chapter 8: Profitability 149

Conclusion 161

Afterword 169

Bibliography 173

Acknowledgments

The Missing Piece is the result of a lifelong journey of self-discovery, which is ironic because that self-discovery would never have happened without the influence of so many people in my life. I am very blessed.

First, I want to thank my mother Sally and my father Bill for your roles in setting the foundation for the man I am today, and for passing along to me so many of your wonderful traits. I'd also like to thank my brother Kirk for being the best guide I ever had, teaching me so many life lessons from a very young age.

Next, my sincere thanks to all the Accelerated Leadership Program participants over the years. Our journeys together form the essence of this book. I truly believe that I have gained as much value as you through our time together. You continually challenged me to create an environment where you could feel safe and supported in your personal and professional growth.

Next, my thanks to Jack Zwissig for taking me under your wing and teaching me so much about human behavior, and how to support others in being the best version of themselves both personally and professionally. So many of the lessons highlighted in this book I learned from you.

Finally, I want to thank my amazing wife, Kelli. You, along with Jack Zwissig, were so instrumental during my early adult life in showing me that it was OK to "feel." Allowing that part of me to re-emerge was a lesson that forever changed the course of my life and enriched my experiences in ways I never could have imagined. Without your involvement, I never would have been able to discover *The Missing Piece*.

Foreword

I have read hundreds of books devoted to leadership and have been mostly disappointed. Typically, they are not useful because they fall into one of two categories: 1) a "catchy" title followed by page after page of name-dropping, or 2) theoretical information that belongs in university classes, not in an organization.

This book is different because Dean embodies *Authentic and Aligned Leadership* and eloquently shares useful principles and examples that can be applied immediately. With the stories he shares of his time in the trenches, and the key steps he takes in creating high-performance cultures, this unique book is worth your time.

If you truly want to find *The Missing Piece* and succeed in all levels of your organization and life, this book is brilliant. In fact, this book, like Dean, is a treasure.

Jack Zwissig
Executive Coach & Senior Facilitator
Pleasanton, California
2021

Introduction

"Culture is what motivates and retains talented employees."
— Betty Thompson

"A leader is one who knows the way, goes the way, and shows the way."
— John C. Maxwell

"Talent wins games, but teamwork and intelligence win championships."
— Michael Jordan

Have you heard this short story before?

Early one morning, a man was walking along the shore after a big storm had passed and found the vast beach littered with starfish, thousands of them stretching in both directions as far as the eye could see.

Off in the distance, the man noticed a young girl approaching. As the girl walked, she paused every so often and as he grew closer, the man could see that she was occasionally bending down to pick up an object and throw it into the sea.

The girl came closer still and the man called out, "Good morning, young lady! May I ask what it is that you are doing?"

The young girl paused, looked up, and replied, "Throwing starfish into the ocean. The tide has washed them up onto the beach and they can't return to the sea by themselves. As the sun rises further, they will die, unless I throw them back into the water."

The man replied, "Why are you doing that? There are thousands of starfish on this beach, and it won't make a difference. They are all going to die."

The girl thought for a moment, then bent down, picked up another starfish, and threw it as far as she could into the ocean. She then turned, smiled, and said, "It made a difference to that one!"

Adapted from "The Star Thrower", by Loren Eiseley (1907-1977)

But What if You Continue the Story?

The starfish story often ends here, omitting some key elements about making a difference. In my version, the story continues:

The young girl then asks the man, "Won't you please help me?"

Inspired by the young girl's vision, the man reaches down, picks up a starfish, and throws it into the ocean.

One by one, and two by two, they continue throwing the starfish back into the sea. Onlookers from the nearby village see what the man and young girl are doing and join in the effort.

Soon, with everyone's help, they save all of the starfish.

My version of this extended story captures the essence of high-performance leadership. The young girl had an idea, a great vision about how to make a difference – saving all of the starfish. She was a role model for acting on that vision, and she influenced and aligned people around her. Soon, she created an effective team – fully engaged, aligned, and collaborating around that vision.

INTRODUCTION

Over my career, I have gained a deep understanding of high-performance leadership and how it all starts with investing in and developing our people. There is so much conversation in today's business world about training and developing personnel; however, I find much of it to be lip service.

Sure, some companies will spend time and money developing the leadership skills of their senior team, but that is only scratching the surface. In fact, that approach typifies *The Missing Piece* in most organizations.

What Is *The Missing Piece*?

High-performance organizations are created by developing an infrastructure of high-performance leaders *at all levels of the organization*. Without such an infrastructure, no single leader can sustain high performance across the enterprise.

Stop for a moment and look at examples in the sports world. Teams that win year after year, sometimes called "dynasties," do so with a combination of aligned ownership, management, coaches, and players. Teams like the New England Patriots, Golden State Warriors, New York Yankees, Manchester United, etc. don't rely on just a few great players. They have high-performance leaders throughout the organization – and they are ALIGNED in purpose, goals, strategies, and implementation.

Many companies take steps toward developing high-performance leaders, though they are often ineffective. I typically have seen half-day and one-day seminars for management development. Mostly, they are didactic in nature and as the old joke goes, "at the end you get a booklet and/or T-shirt as a reward for not sleeping through the PowerPoint presentations." Obviously, some are better than others, but either way they are all short-term learning, not mastery of new thinking and new skills.

These short-term modular workshops in and of themselves don't address the long-term development of an organization's NEXT senior managers. And if organizations aren't building their bench, WHO will lead us in the future? HOW will they lead us?

This is a critical area of focus because without it, an organization must "hope" they are ready when the time for new leadership arrives. Or the organization must "hope" high-performance executives can be successfully brought into the company. I have always adhered to the adage that "hope" is a poor strategy.

That is why I refer to high-performance leadership at all levels of the organization as *The Missing Piece*.

Filling In *The Missing Piece*

So, why is *The Missing Piece* largely ignored? Perhaps companies fear that they are spending money to train senior managers only to raise their profile for others who are shopping for talented executives.

I personally love the cartoon drawing I saw in a business publication. The image was titled "The Corporate Dilemma" and featured two executives arguing about training their employees. The CFO said to the CEO, "But what if we spend the time and money training our people and they leave?" to which the CEO replied, "What if we don't train them and they stay?" The truth is, in my experience, employees whose companies invest in their personal development feel a heightened sense of loyalty and are far less eager to jump ship.

I am not just speaking here of traditional *management training*, such as time management, assigning tasks, and performance reviews; I am referring to creating an open, authentic culture and inspiring collaboration across the organization, which in turn will increase the creativity and

INTRODUCTION

innovation of the entire enterprise, leading not only to optimal results, but to a fully-engaged and loyal workforce as well.

Learning About Leadership at an Early Age

In my youth, my brother Kirk was a bully; at least he was to me. During those years, I lived in a constant state of fear. While in his own way he taught me so much about life, I retreated into a shell of self-preservation and became an introvert. In my situation, I decided it was better to be seen and not heard. In fact, I actually decided it was sometimes better not to be seen at all.

My father had a very strong presence, which added to my early challenges. I felt he was difficult to approach, and it was difficult growing up in his shadow. Unfortunately, before I really had a chance to get out of my father's shadow, he passed away – he was only 47 and I was 13. Not having him around in my teens was difficult, to say the least. He could have been such a source of wisdom and inspiration to me as I approached adulthood.

Transformation at Lifespring

In my early twenties, I felt I was just meandering my way through life. I was smart and a good student, and I believed I was on a path to success, but I was numb. Something was missing for me, but I couldn't put my finger on it. Then, I was lucky enough to come across a personal growth program offered by a company called Lifespring. In today's world, Lifespring would be considered a form of emotional intelligence training.

I participated in two Lifespring five-day workshops and learned more about myself—my true self—than I had discovered in my life up to that point. I learned about the real value I bring to this world, and how I could make a difference.

In the advanced training, I met Jack Zwissig, who is not only one of my best friends today, but also one of the most impassioned, intuitive, and caring people I have ever met. After I had been numb for so long, he taught me that it was OK to *feel* – a lesson that changed my life.

I learned about openness and authenticity, and I experienced an awakening as I gained a deep understanding of human connection. I learned about both myself and others, and I realized that I was much more than just my intellect. In fact, I came to learn and live by a quote from Teddy Roosevelt: "No one cares how much you know until they know how much you care."

I worked for Lifespring for one year (1980-81), and was able to continue my "self-actualization," which to me is really just a process of continual improvement. While working for Lifespring, I met Kelli Frisinger who, unbeknownst to me at the time, would be my wife in two short years (and would remain my amazing wife for 38 years to date).

Lifespring gave us a common foundation of being real and genuine. Kelli was so alive and energetic, and she challenged me to be authentic all the time. Kelli is my life source and my best friend.

We used our common foundation as an approach for raising our children. We wanted them to be authentic, caring, and honest – not just intellectually honest, but also emotionally honest. Kelli and I worked hard to stay emotionally close to them. I believe we did a really great job – they are two incredibly genuine people.

My Introduction to the 'Real World'

As I started my public accounting career in 1981 with Ernst & Whinney (now EY), I began to realize that the lessons I had recently learned—and was continuing to learn—about human connection and impacting people were just as relevant in business as in my personal life. I realized my impact would be determined far less by my individual performance than by the performance of the teams I led.

Without this understanding I had gained about human development, I don't believe I would have been on a successful career path. Integrating these lessons into my daily personal and professional life took many years – mostly because I was bringing these learnings into business, and they were not inherent in the cultures of the organizations where I worked.

As I continued to navigate my career, completing my public accounting stint at Ernst, stepping in as Group Controller for a recreational and industrial products manufacturer, and entering the entertainment industry at Disney, I repeatedly came across the same phenomenon – *The Missing Piece!* In my opinion, none of these companies was taking the time to build a high-performance culture by developing high-performance leaders at all levels of their organization.

Growing Fox After Ground Zero

I arrived at 20th Century Fox three weeks after 9/11. The studio was in full austerity mode and the training and development budget had effectively been cut to zero. I saw a tremendous number of really smart people, but I also saw a tremendous opportunity to increase the level of high-performance leadership behavior.

I quickly realized that the Fox culture was very entrepreneurial – which for me was good news and bad. First, the bad news. There was minimal central infrastructure in the organization, meaning any significant personnel development plan would need to be driven through grassroots efforts. At Fox, like at many companies, managers were expected to learn leadership skills on their own.

So, here again was *The Missing Piece.*

The good news? The less rigid infrastructure left much room for bringing forth new ideas and approaches, and I saw an opportunity to expand beyond my traditional CFO responsibilities and play a role in building effective leadership teams.

It was here that I really immersed myself in personnel development. After initiating some workshops with our senior team and generating increased levels of trust and collaboration, I started thinking about how to build a Fox Studio finance bench.

I started small. I selected just four or five finance managers and met with them weekly. It was a very informal program at first, if it was a program at all. I just worked to connect with them, establish a relationship, and give them more context about our overall business.

I shared openly with them about everything, including industry challenges, company strategy, and office politics. We did some exercises that demonstrated how to give and receive feedback and how to support team members in being their best. We met over a six- to nine-month period, and at the end each cohort they did a project together – to build their connection, work through their issues, and add some value to the company. Early projects included broad topics like Recruiting and Retention and Cost Efficiencies.

I developed this early program using skills I gained during my years of personal development and honed during my roles with prior employers. The concepts were the same, though I needed to make some slight adjustments for applications in the business world.

I hosted three program cycles within Finance, and then HR approached me and said, "This program is too good to offer only to Finance. You need to lead this program for the whole studio."

INTRODUCTION

This felt a bit risky to me at first. I had been developing my own people, and we had been doing experiential exercises utilizing the Discovery Model – a model that allows participants to experience new behaviors and approaches at a deep level.

If someone in Finance had an issue with the nature of any of the activities, they would talk to me. However, if I led this program for the whole studio, I would then have potential complaints going to any of the studio division presidents. The last thing I wanted was a division president to come to me and ask, "What are you doing to my people?"

Yet, I knew the underlying value of these Discovery Model exercises and expanding the program was worth the risk. I worked with HR to provide a bit more structure and formality to these long-established exercises, and we set it up as a nine-month program. The first three months brought the cohort together, gave them a foundation for collaborative leadership, and built a level of mutual trust and respect. The second three months focused on tools and exercises for participants to push each other to be their best, and really built a level of group accountability and responsibility. The final three months included presentations to senior management with participants making recommendations on challenges and opportunities facing the company and the industry.

Overall, I spent 17 years at Fox building leadership in teams throughout the organization. Ultimately, we witnessed an incredibly effective development model for creating an open, collaborative culture where creativity and innovation thrive. I wrote this book to share what I learned, including what worked and what didn't.

Speed Up Your Success

I decided to write this book for the same reason I started Hallett Leadership: so that others could grasp the lessons I learned much faster than I did. I want to share the secrets of developing a high-performance culture with leaders who truly want to take their organizations to the next level.

Too often we tell ourselves that if we can just get past our current roadblocks and jump over a few more hurdles, we will take the time to build and integrate a program to fully develop our teams, but we just don't ever seem to get there.

I thought about writing this book as a parable. Yet, while a parable is easy to understand and can teach us valuable lessons, I too often find that everything just falls too neatly into place as the story evolves. Unfortunately, life and business are not always that easy, and real life is messy – but the underlying lessons are simple.

In this book, I share the story of building the 20th Century Fox digital supply chain, ultimately renamed the Fox Media Framework. I led the project utilizing the accelerated leadership techniques I share in this book. In the end, the Fox Media Framework was an incredible success, transforming the way Fox created, replicated, and distributed media throughout the world, though there were many trials and tribulations along the way. I believe it is important to share both the successes and failures of our efforts to truly demonstrate the power of transformation and culture change in an organization.

I also include some "Leadership Close Encounters." All leadership leaves a wake, and I believe it is critical to see the long-term impact some leadership actions and techniques can have on individuals and the team.

The Path to High Performance

Over the years, I learned that true leadership development can be so meaningful. Yet, as I worked my way through my career, I saw that most companies limited development of their people to technical training. And when the good, individual technical performers were elevated to management roles, no one had invested adequate time and resources to prepare them to *lead and manage.*

As I said earlier, I knew they went to some management trainings and learned about time management, administering performance reviews, and other managerial techniques, but no one spoke to them about true leadership, empowering their teams, and working with each other to be their very best.

Over time, I learned what high-performance leadership was, including what being open, authentic, empowering, inspiring, and honest was all about. And I learned that for organizations to be truly high-performance, they need to drive high-performance leadership at all levels of the organization: *The Missing Piece.*

The Accelerated Leadership Program

During my time at Fox, I had great support from many people in addressing *The Missing Piece.* Using the skills I developed over the first 20 years of my career, we began developing managers into the high performers of today and the great leaders of tomorrow.

Similar to the program at Fox, the Accelerated Leadership Program (ALP) that is now the key offering at my company, Hallett Leadership, is founded on the leadership skills I learned early and honed over the course of my career. ALP is the world's premier leadership training program, the principles and Discovery Model exercises of which have decades of proven results. The program creates an arena for forging collaborative, high-performance leadership from within the ranks of an organization over the course of nine months. The curriculum includes integrating the knowledge and learnings from the program into the cohort's daily work activities, which ultimately becomes the driving force in elevating company culture into high performance.

The nine-month ALP curriculum, which takes place while participants continue to perform in their current roles, allows true changes in behavior and mastery of new thinking and new skills.

Now, for the first time, ALP is available to you and your organization. Together, we can fill in your organization's *Missing Piece*!

This book shares stories and provides insights on how truly developing your team will shift your organizational culture and raise performance to a whole new level. So, take the "hope" strategy off the table. Your company's journey to high performance can begin today!

Chapter 1

The Importance of People

> *"The business of business is people."*
> — Herb Kelleher

> *"You don't build a business. You build people and then the people build the business."*
> — Zig Ziglar

> *"We are not in the coffee business serving people. We are in the people business serving coffee."*
> — Howard Schultz

While at 20th Century Fox—in the early days of true video on demand (VOD)—we were negotiating deals to license our movies and television shows to outlets around the world in a digital format. Until this time, all of our movie and television elements were stored on film or on videotape. One day, Peter Chernin, the CEO of the Fox Group, approached me and said, "We are negotiating and closing VOD deals around the world. Are you going to be prepared to provide those platforms with digital versions of our films and TV shows?"

Peter was asking a great question. Fox had a very entrepreneurial culture with vertically structured divisions. We didn't have much in the way of centralized support groups connecting the different verticals. We had Theatrical Distribution. We had Home Entertainment. We had Television Distribution.

Left to their own devices, each division independently would likely have taken its analog supply chain and converted it into its own digital supply chain. We would have ended up with at least three different supply chains, which would have been incredibly inefficient in the world of digital media, and Peter knew it.

I went to the film studio chairman and said, "I think this is an area where I can add a lot of value. It doesn't make any sense for us to develop three different supply chains. Instead, let me lead this process to establish a single, studio-wide solution." He agreed. He didn't give me the power of a public mandate, but he supported me in driving the process forward.

A couple of years earlier, I had led another Fox initiative to establish our strategy for the rollout of Digital Cinema. For months I had watched as the industry struggled to align around a strategy for theaters to migrate from traditional film projectors to digital cinema projectors. I sat in one large meeting after another witnessing very little in terms of forward momentum. There were simply too many stakeholders unwilling to bend on their demands. In the struggle, I saw an opportunity for Fox to step up and establish an industry-wide Digital Cinema rollout solution. I knew from experience that we would need a skilled, effective team to accomplish such a monumental task, so I worked on a game plan to bring in the best and brightest stakeholders from around the studio to kick off the project, and then…

I used the tactic that Quincy Jones used during the recording of "We Are the World" – gathering the leaders of each function (IT, Sales, Engineering, etc.), and instructing them to "check their egos at the door." I asked each leader to bring a list of their "must-haves" to our meeting, and informed them that we weren't leaving the room until we were aligned around a strategy.

THE IMPORTANCE OF PEOPLE

In that meeting, which ran several hours, we hammered out a new Digital Cinema strategy that held up not only for Fox, but for the entire industry rollout that lasted nearly a decade.

With the Digital Cinema experience under my belt, I felt confident I could effectively lead the Fox effort to establish our studio-wide digital supply chain. When I started down this path, little did I know I was embarking on a multi-year journey that would provide never-ending tests of my leadership skills and ability to achieve great things through teams.

In 1979, at age 21, my best friend Ralph and I were heading to Airborne Eddie's Freestyle Ski Camp in Canada. For a year, we had planned this trip. We would leave Los Angeles on Sunday morning for a road trip through California, Oregon, Washington, and Idaho, arriving in British Columbia to ski and train for a week with the world's top freestyle ski competitors. At the time we planned the trip, I didn't realize that Ralph would end up enrolling in what today would be considered an emotional intelligence training program called Lifespring, or that his graduation would take place in Los Angeles the day *after* our originally scheduled departure. I vividly recall my frustration in delaying the beginning of our ski excursion by one day because now we would have to drive nonstop for 30 hours to reach our destination in time.

However, that frustration pales in comparison to the revelations I had as we took turns at the wheel in the small cockpit of my 1974 Porsche 914. Little did I know the nature of the training that Ralph had just experienced. During our 30-hour expedition, I witnessed a transformation in Ralph that I had never seen before. My best friend, whom I had known like the back of my own hand, was suddenly embracing a new joy for life and exhibiting an incredibly authentic belief in himself. I was so taken with his transformation that by the time we arrived in

Canada, I was already signed up to attend my own Lifespring training the following month, and the timing couldn't have been better.

Lifespring and the Start of My Transformation

I had been looking for more out of life than the existence I was experiencing. Sure, I had a lot going for me. I was a rising senior at the University of Southern California. (OK, it was much easier to get in back then!) And I already had locked up my internship with one of the Big 8 accounting firms. Plus, I was on my way to freestyle camp! I should have been ecstatic about my life, but I wasn't. I didn't feel connected to people at a fundamental level, and I wasn't sure why. Deep down, I knew there had to be more.

I had spent time with a psychologist looking for a deeper understanding of life and my place in the world. Through my discussions with him, I learned something that I really already knew – that I was not the best at expressing my emotions and sharing what was going on inside, and I learned how that could inhibit my ability to connect with others. This insight was the catalyst I needed, but the progress seemed slow to me. Working with the psychologist, I learned more about what made me tick and how I could evolve and grow, but I was impatient. I wanted to accelerate the process. This five-day Lifespring training seemed like the perfect springboard.

Lifespring was my first exposure to the Discovery Model for learning, in which I had the opportunity to experience different parts of me in action – parts I had denied for a long time. I participated in many exercises. Some were in large groups, some in small groups, others in dyads, and still others in guided meditation. These exercises allowed me to discover my inner self – what I have learned over the years to be my true, authentic self. I connected with my natural leadership abilities, learned what value I have in the world, engaged with my interpersonal talents and abilities, expanded my communication skills, and experienced connection with others on an entirely new level.

I always knew I was smart and great with numbers, but for the first time ever—or at least for the first time since I was a child—I realized there was so much more to *me*. I learned so much about myself (self-awareness) and how to connect with others (authenticity).

My Inner Awakening

One of the most impactful exercises for me was a feedback process in which each participant in the program assessed everyone else's level of participation. I had always been a nice guy, and most people were kind to me, yet all these people felt I was holding back, and they were right!

In my youth, I had formed beliefs about myself based on my early childhood (I will share more about that a bit later) – beliefs that definitely limited my confidence and self-esteem. Suddenly, with the feedback I was receiving, I realized how much my feeling of "I don't matter" was in the way of my connecting with other people. It was crystal clear to me that my playing it safe for so long was preventing me from having the human connection I so desperately wanted. That was truly a transformational moment, a true awakening, and a turning point in the trajectory of my life. I am certainly no Maslow, but that moment sent me on a lifetime journey of enlightenment and self-discovery.

Later in the same program, there was another exercise where I had the opportunity to take center stage and communicate one-on-one with a number of individuals, one after another, at a level deeper than I remember ever experiencing up to that point in my life. I had the opportunity to speak to their most admirable characteristics that they had not yet fully embraced – personal power, commitment, self-worth, and vulnerability. Surprisingly, these were the same characteristics I had been struggling to embrace myself. I saw so much of me in them. I learned about this phenomenon referred to as the "mirror concept" and realized that in life we often teach best what we most need to learn.

It was in those moments that I grasped a real sense of my own personal power for the very first time. I learned how I could use that personal power to connect with people and impact them in an incredibly positive way.

It took me many years to integrate these lessons so that my external actions truly aligned with my internal self (authentic leadership), but I realized I was much more than just a numbers guy. I understood the strength and value of my own emotional intelligence. I learned how to tap into my inner self and connect with people on a much deeper level than ever before. The human connection I had craved all my life was now all around me. I also realized just how valuable such a connection was for business and that I could apply these lessons there.

Emotional Intelligence

In 1995, author Daniel Goleman came out with a bestselling book called *Emotional Intelligence*. Even though the term had been used in psychology circles since the 1960s, the popularity of Goleman's book took the concept mainstream. Essentially, emotional intelligence, sometimes referred to as emotional quotient (EQ), boils down to empathy and awareness. It speaks to greater understanding, deeper relationships, and more efficient leadership skills.

Key components of greater emotional intelligence include active listening, asking perceptive questions, being aware of body language and tonality, perfecting word choice, and assuming positive intent within relationships.

In his book, Goleman writes:

> *People's emotions are rarely put into words; far more often they are expressed through other cues. The key to intuiting another's feelings is in the ability to read nonverbal channels, tone of voice, gesture, facial expression and the like....*[1]

Goleman goes on to say:

> *Leadership is not domination, but the art of persuading people to work toward a common goal....*[2]

In his subsequent book, *Social Intelligence*, Goleman adds:

> *... Self-absorption in all its forms kills empathy, let alone compassion. When we focus on ourselves, our world contracts as our problems and preoccupations loom large. But when we focus on others, our world expands. Our own problems drift to the periphery of the mind and so seem smaller, and we increase our capacity for connection—or compassionate action.*[3]

As you can see, emotional intelligence offers valuable insights to managers, teachers, counselors, and anyone who works with others. Through these insights, these leaders can impact the workplace culture.

---

1 Daniel Goleman, *Emotional Intelligence: Why It Can Matter More Than IQ* (New York, NY: Bantam Books, 2006) 86.
2 Goleman, *Emotional Intelligence*, 133.
3 Daniel Goleman, *Social Intelligence* (New York, NY: Bantam Books, 2006) 54.

Leadership Close Encounter — The Disingenuous

Several major media companies have experienced periods of tremendous growth. At one of these media conglomerates, there were two leaders at the top. One leader had a million ideas while the other tended to be more pragmatic and rational. The former would walk into a room and throw out a number of his ideas – some great, some not so great. Then, when he would leave the room, the latter would inform the team which ideas to act on and which to ignore.

That balance was critical to the effectiveness of this media company until the pragmatic leader left the organization. Once the creative leader was alone at the helm, with his unfettered ideas, he constrained the power and authority of his divisional chairmen. He gave tremendous power to his central strategy team, preventing the divisional leaders from launching any significant initiatives without the direct involvement of his office.

When the company was in a growth cycle, the central strategy team was able to focus on launching new businesses that did not compete with the existing divisions, and the process worked quite well. However, when growth tapered off, the central strategy folks turned their focus inward and imposed themselves on the existing businesses. Their message felt to me like "We are smarter than you and better than you. Give us the information and get out of our way."

Divisional leaders did what they could to keep the central strategy team out of their hair. As a result, some people in that group took to a disingenuous approach. Some members of that team would verbally agree to work in partnership, apparently only to serve their goal of extracting information from the business units. Once they had the information they wanted, they would carve the executives (including me) out of the initiatives, stating that these were corporate initiatives, and therefore business unit executives could not be a part of them.

This approach resulted in business units building walls around their organizations, causing a lack of proactive collaboration across business unit verticals. It was not a healthy culture.

The Culture Flywheel

Throughout my career, I discovered most organizations don't dedicate time and resources to work on their culture. I developed the Culture Flywheel as a model that can be used to establish and maintain a healthy framework for teaching the principles I'm sharing in this book.

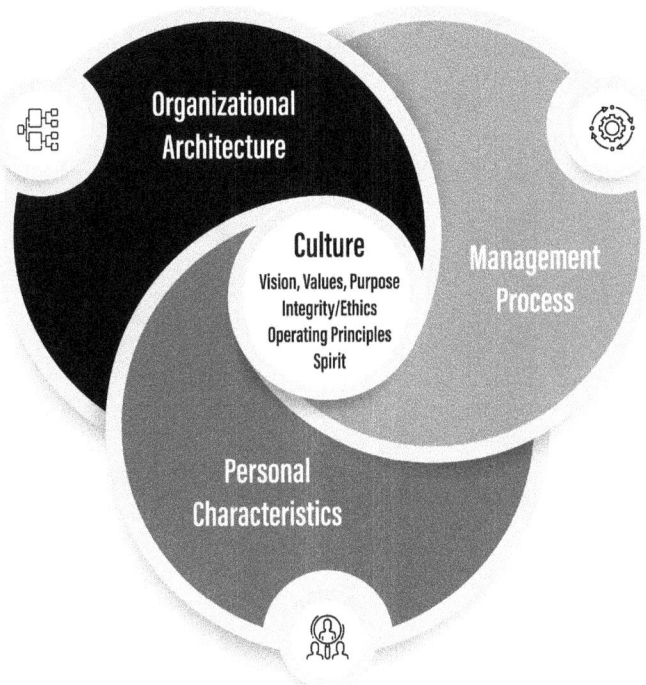

In an organization with a healthy culture, all of the surrounding elements in the Culture Flywheel work together – people (personal characteristics), structure, and processes. An organization that organizes and aligns its people and implements processes to support the functioning of a new organizational culture becomes nimble and capable of responding quickly to changes in the marketplace and regulatory environment. Even more importantly, such nimble and responsive cultures can actually initiate and drive key industry changes.

A Case Study from Fox

When I arrived at Fox, the film studio operated similarly to other major studios: as a number of successful vertical divisions. Each film moved through the organization in a sequential manner, launching in the theatrical window, then moving to Home Entertainment, and then TV Distribution. There were also films with consumer product tie-ins, video games, and other related content.

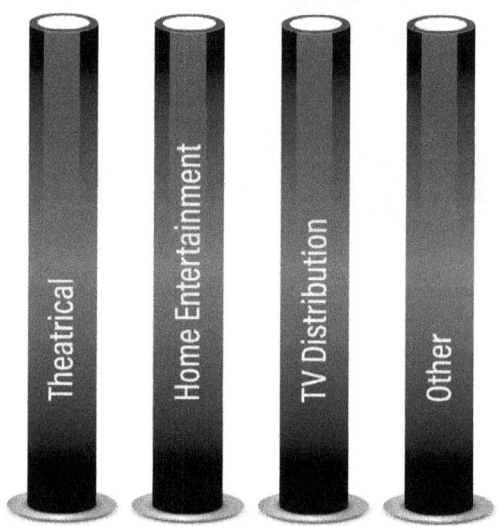

Having each of these primary and ancillary business units operate in an independent fashion did not necessarily maximize the potential value of the underlying intellectual property. There were additional opportunities available, which Fox pursued over the years by creating horizontal connective tissue across the verticals.

An example of this connective tissue was Fox establishing a brand and franchise management group, thereby modifying the organizational structure. Similarly, strategy, marketing, and supply chain groups were established to provide further connections and synergy across the aisles.

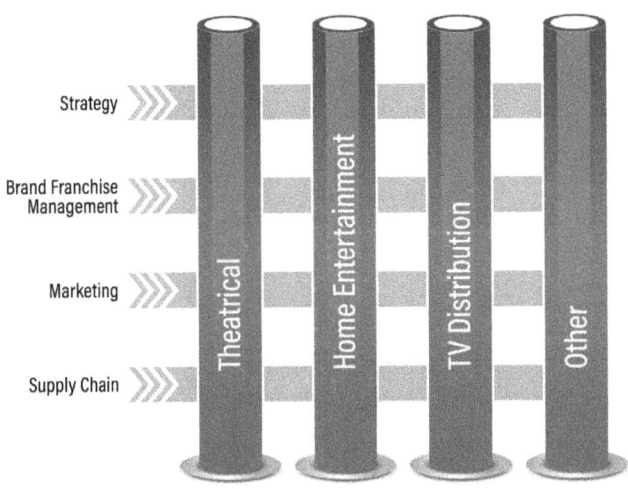

Changing the organizational structure, the top-left element on the Flywheel, and establishing these modified groups was not enough. The top-right element of the Flywheel, the processes, needed to be changed to integrate the new horizontal groups into the operations of the various vertical divisions. For example, a cross-divisional supply chain group would be completely ineffective without changing the underlying supply chain processes of each of the affected divisions. Similarly, a brand management group would be hard-pressed to add value without being included in a film's pre-production process, identifying opportunities to broaden the reach of the intellectual property.

Through these cross-divisional efforts, ideas could be shared, and operations could be streamlined for the benefit of the entire organization. Once the structure and processes were adjusted, the bottom, foundational element of the Flywheel—the people—had to be aligned as well.

People Are an Organization's Most Valuable Asset

Sure, the Culture Flywheel shows that the component parts form an integrated organism, but without the people, you can build the best organizational structure, design the best processes, and still never get off the ground. The people must be aligned and engaged.

Research from the National Association of Business Owners & Entrepreneurs reports:

> *It has been well documented that employees who feel valued and engaged are 24% more likely to increase sales… 50% post messages, pictures, and videos about employers on social, and 33% have shared unsolicited praise or positive comments… But it goes beyond that and to the core of what any business exists to accomplish: satisfy their customer so that they generate repeat and referral sales.*[4]

Alignment; communication and collaboration; teamwork; and creativity and innovation—everything that we're going to cover in this book—will help your organization. But by starting with the important foundation of people, you will set your organization up for achieving greater heights of profitability and success.

In our techno-driven society, many entrepreneurs and executives feel that all they need to do is build a killer app, and then the world will flock to their door. Maybe that is true. Maybe not. Just think about how many organizations you have witnessed build the killer app and then disintegrate from within. Companies like Uber and WeWork have experienced a great deal of turbulence because they didn't have the right people in the right spots on the bus, to use the analogy from Jim Collins' book *Good to Great*.

---

[4] Ines LeBow, "The Importance of People in Business Success." NABOE, October 9, 2017. https://www.naboe.org/importance-people-business-success/

That's the #1 lesson I have learned in all my years – *It's the People!* You may have the killer app or the killer brand, but if you don't cultivate the right culture with your people, your business likely will eventually come crumbling down. It is the people who define an organization. It is the people who drive the conversation, the social direction, and therefore the business direction. Without the investment and buy-in (alignment) of the people, the organization is irrelevant and out of sync.

Seeing Firsthand the Results of Great People at Fox

When I came to Fox in 2001, there was no development budget due to austerity right after 9/11. We had a lot of really smart people, but we were not actively developing enough of them as high-performance leaders. The HR team arranged opportunities for us to hear thought leaders speak on various approaches to leadership, which I believe always provides some value; however, most of what we heard was forgotten as soon as we faced our next crisis. We needed something more. I reached out to our VP of Human Resources and informed her that I knew a leadership facilitator who could bring hands-on leadership skills to Fox – and she was all ears.

We arranged for a series of two-day workshops. We started with senior executives, including our chairmen, and set the tone from the top. This approach had a monumental impact throughout the organization. The chairmen were espousing the value of leadership and setting the example that we all had room to improve, and that spoke volumes. By the time the senior executives completed the third two-day workshop, we could see dramatic changes in the nature of the interactions across the top level of our organization.

We then brought similar training offerings to the middle management group and built upon that year after year. We had committed to purposely develop and train our people, and the increase in teamwork and collaboration was significant. As a result, we were able to take the company to new heights. It was no accident that we achieved eight consecutive record-breaking years, and nine out of ten. Sure, we developed and released great product, but it all started with our people.

Your people are your foundation. That's why it is so important you start with the priority of your people; it is always about the people. People are the most valuable asset in every business.

Chapter 2

Authentic Leadership

"No one cares how much you know until they know how much you care."
— Theodore Roosevelt

"Vulnerability is not weakness; it's our greatest measure of courage."
— Brené Brown

"We all need people who will give us feedback. That's how we improve."
— Bill Gates

I knew immediately that taking the lead on the digital supply chain, which came to be known as the Fox Media Framework, was no small task, especially without a mandate.

While I was at The Walt Disney Company in 1998, we launched an enterprise-wide shared services initiative, the scope of which included filmed entertainment, television, theme parks, and consumer products. At the time, I was the senior vice president of Planning and Control, and I represented the studio on the initiative's Steering Committee.

After a preliminary feasibility study, Tom Staggs, the Corporate CFO, appointed me as the Executive Sponsor for Shared Services, meaning I would run point for the enterprise-wide initiative.

I must admit that, at the time, it felt like Tom had asked for volunteers, and everyone else took one step back, leaving me standing alone. But then Tom made a bold statement that was incredibly empowering. He said, "Dean is the Executive Sponsor for Shared Services. I trust him in this role, and whatever he decides is final. There is no avenue of appeal."

On the one hand, having that mandate was a great thing. I knew it could give me leverage to break through unnecessary resistance. If people knew that there was no avenue of appeal, but saw my willingness to sit down with them, really wanting to understand the issues relevant to their business, then they'd see the way that I work and appreciate it. Without the mandate, they might always believe that if they pushed hard on me long enough, they'd win.

On the other hand, even with the stated mandate, I knew I had my challenges ahead of me. You see, I had the authority to make decisions on behalf of the entire Walt Disney Company, but I was still a studio executive and any decision I made could be perceived as having a studio bias. So, I was very careful to be open and honest, and as objective as possible in making the best decisions I could on behalf of the overall organization. I kept the corporate mandate in my back pocket to be used only if absolutely necessary.

Fast-forward to Fox. Now I was leading a digital supply chain initiative without such a mandate. I knew instinctively what that meant, as I had experienced these situations countless times during my career. While I could do all my homework and lay out a very objective case for moving in a particular direction, I was subject to all kinds of internal bias, second-guessing, and territorialism.

My instincts were correct. Our efforts were regularly met with high levels of resistance. In fact, in many cases, once we created alignment around a decision, I would find that after a week or two of others pushing their own agendas, the alignment had dissipated, and we were starting from scratch.

In terms of the existing physical supply chains, the various Fox divisions had been operating for decades in their own silos, and it had worked extremely well for them. Just speaking of a studio-wide digital supply chain was incredibly threatening to the status quo. Stakeholders were locked into their fixed beliefs and fixed behaviors regarding how things should work. It was completely understandable. For decades, each of these businesses had controlled their own processes from A to Z.

Their supply chain functions, which included sales servicing—delivering the physical media to customers—were deeply integrated into their sales functions. In fact, some divisions believed that every sales servicing encounter was in fact another opportunity to sell. So, the last thing they wanted was some sort of centralized group getting in the middle of their business. The past had informed them that they were the best at their business and would be better served by managing all the components themselves.

This behavior was actually buoyed by the unspoken Fox mantra that came from the top and had driven tremendous success for years: "Do whatever you have to do for your business to be successful." That approach granted license to divisions to keep others out of their hair. That was going to make this process incredibly challenging. Some of the divisions believed the old manner of doing things in the analog world was still the right way to go.

Many individuals in those divisions would look for any evidence they could get their hands on to prove they were right, even though we were moving into a digital arena that was new to all of us. When we move into a new area, <u>we don't know what we don't know</u>, and we start making decisions based on an illusion of certainty. When we do this, we typically are not open to hearing others' perspectives. This was definitely what I was feeling as we launched this initiative.

Early in our process, one high-level division executive exclaimed that if I pursued the design, development, and implementation of a studio-wide digital supply chain, I would actually destroy their business. This executive asked me, "Are you suggesting we separate Sales from Sales Servicing?" to which I replied with an emphatic "Yes!" Delivering the media, whether in physical or digital form, would definitely be part of the supply chain. Without it, there would be no supply chain. The executive's response to me was simply, "With all due respect, Dean, you've never been in sales!"

This didn't bother me all that much. When I led Shared Services at Disney, I heard claims all over the company about how critical it was for each division to control its own processes, even something as straightforward as payroll. At that time, the Disney Stores actually spoke the loudest, claiming that losing the payroll function would completely undermine their business. As I said before, I had a mandate in my back pocket, but I didn't want to just blindly play that card.

So, I met with the Disney Stores senior management and listened to their apprehensions. I wanted to be transparent with them and be sure I wasn't missing anything. As it turned out, they had some real concerns – but they didn't involve payroll. The Disney Stores were retail businesses that were quite dispersed geographically, and they had fairly high employee turnover. Their concern was having local human resource teams that could deal with employee issues, including hiring and terminations. Shared Services wasn't touching any of that.

After our meeting, the Disney Stores agreed that there were no operational concerns in moving to a shared services payroll model. We all left there aligned about what they really needed, and their management felt heard and supported. Even though I didn't use the mandate, it was a great thing to have because a mandate helps maintain a constructive dialog. Others know *you have the right to pull the trigger – they know they can't just push on you endlessly.*

At Fox, I explained to my studio chairman that someday in the not-too-distant future, one of the high-level division executives would likely storm into the chairman's office and tell him that if he allowed me to continue my approach for developing an enterprise-wide digital supply chain, I would destroy their business. The chairman chuckled and said not to worry – I had his support. Of course, support and mandate are two different things.

We were on our way, but this was going to be a long journey.

My first professional role after college was as a staff accountant with one of the top accounting firms – Ernst & Whinney (now EY) in Los Angeles. My father, William "Bill" Hallett, had worked at Ernst during my youth, and I had developed solid relationships with the "old guard" partners there, so I had some connections going in on Day One. These partners told me that had my father not passed, he would have been tapped as the Managing Partner of the entire firm. While that feedback about my father and his legacy warmed my heart, I knew that meant I had huge shoes to fill. At the time, I believed I would be a lifer at Ernst. I believed I would work my way up to partner level, spending my entire career with the firm.

The environment in my early days at Ernst was a positive one, with lots of teamwork and specialists contributing in their areas of expertise. Over time, however, the old guard began retiring, and during my fifth year the firm brought in new leadership from around the country. Under the influence of one of these new leaders, whom I will call Tim, the culture (not a word I used back then) in our office began to change.

I felt tension early on as Tim seemed to respond to virtually any suggestion or request I made with immediate resistance and opposition. I had no idea what was driving the resistance, so I continued reaching out to build a relationship and connect with him – to no avail. Up to this point, my track record had been rock-solid, and I had received stellar reviews along the way, demonstrating that I produced high-quality results. Something just didn't feel right, but I couldn't put my finger on it.

Revealing the Heart Issue

I began to feel disconnected from the organization, and I could feel my level of engagement dropping. Then, one day I gained a crystal-clear view of what was behind Tim's opposition. Tim was spending a week escorting his boss, the firm's overall Managing Partner—Ray—on client visits. Ray was the firm's first new overall Managing Partner since my father's death. I was the manager on the engagement with the Times Mirror Company, one of our office's top clients, and on this given day, Ray was paying us a visit at the Times Mirror offices.

Mike, the Times Mirror engagement partner, introduced Ray to the team, and introduced me as Bill Hallett's son. Ray, realizing who I was, immediately became emotional and reached out to me in a full embrace – and over his shoulder I could see Tim turn beet red with anger. Suddenly, it hit me. I realized all of the resistance and obstruction I had felt from Tim emanated from his belief that I was receiving special treatment solely based on my father's achievements.

Tim's view, albeit a flawed one, was influenced by his own belief system and limitations. It truly had nothing to do with me, but his perception was his own reality. He had not taken the effort to look at my performance objectively or get input from others with whom I had great working relationships. Instead, he was intent on frustrating my efforts, which ultimately led to my decision to leave the firm. Upon my departure, I shared my story with several of the partners, and each of them confirmed my suspicions about the reason for Tim's actions.

This was the first time in my career that I had found myself in a culture where I felt I could no longer thrive – it was a pivotal moment for me.

I regularly advise people to find a culture that supports who they are and allows them to thrive. If you cannot thrive in your current culture, see what you can do to influence and change that culture. Ultimately, though, if the culture is not a fit, make a change. Life is short.

Often times we wait for senior leadership to drive a change in organizational culture from the top. The truth is we all have the ability to influence the culture around us, whether it be the culture of our department, our division, our segment, or the entire company. We have the power to enroll others to be more open and collaborative, and to foster an environment where teamwork is encouraged and team members push each other to be their best.

I strived to influence the culture in Ernst's Los Angeles office, but ultimately, I realized it was time for me to move on. My vision of being a lifelong partner with the firm was no more.

Perception Is Reality

Tim's view reminds me of an Indian folktale I heard decades ago. Once upon a time in India, a group of blind Hindu monks heard that a strange new animal called an elephant had been brought to their village, but none of the monks was aware of its size, shape, or form. Out of curiosity, they said, "We must inspect the elephant and know it by touch." They then went to visit the elephant, and each monk stretched out his arm to feel it.

The first blind monk, whose hand landed on the elephant's trunk, said, "This animal is like a thick snake." The second monk, whose hand reached its ear, said it seemed like a fan. The third blind monk, whose hand was on its leg, said, "No, the elephant is a pillar, like a tree." The fourth monk placed his hand upon the elephant's side and declared it felt like a wall, while the fifth grabbed its tail and described it as a rope. Finally, the sixth blind monk touched its tusk. He stated that everyone else was wrong and that "The elephant feels smooth and sharp like a spear."

This story exemplifies how our perception is always limited. We need the culmination of each other's perspectives to draw a clear picture of the truth. When I'm training executives in a workshop or coaching them on-site, I'll often present the diagram below:

PERCEPTUAL RELATIVITY

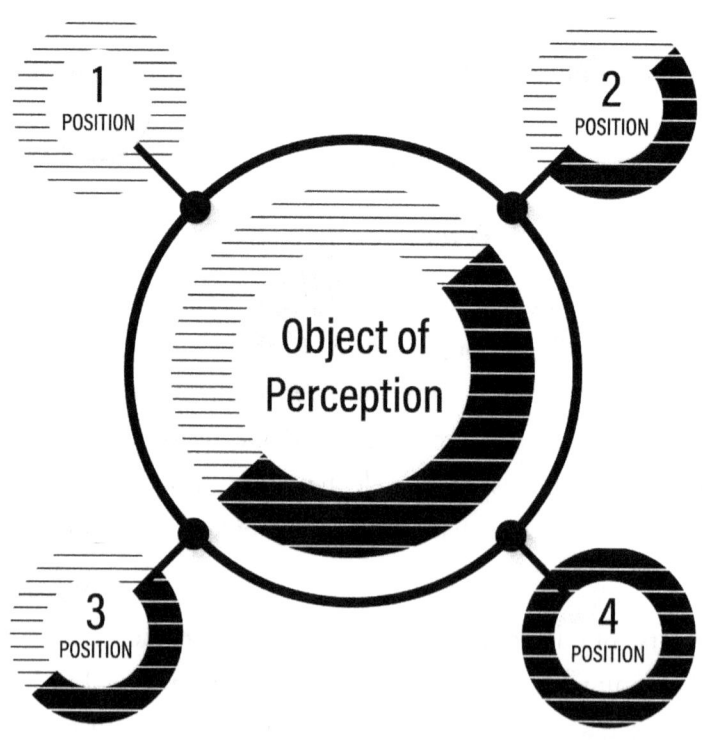

The point at which a person is standing relative to the location of the object of perception directly impacts what the person sees. For example, the person in Position 1 only sees the light side of the object. The person in Position 4 only sees the dark side of the object. And each of the individuals in Positions 2 and 3 sees a different view of the object that appears to be 50% light and 50% dark. I call this "Perceptual Reality," and it's the same principle illustrated in the story of the blind monks and the elephant.

Many people mistakenly believe their own narrow perception is reality, but the truth is you get a much more accurate picture of how things *really are* when you seek out the perspectives of others. Authentic leaders want to hear others' perspectives. They are comfortable knowing they cannot see everything themselves, and that they don't have all the answers. The lesson is if you don't consider other people's perspectives during your leadership journey, you'll basically be leading blind. You will never have a full picture of your options or lead your organization to reach its ultimate potential.

Self-Awareness Is the Key to Authenticity

When a manager moves higher up the leadership chain of an organization, they can feel threatened by other people's perspectives. They also tend to fear failure, seek perfection, and assume they need to have all the answers. None of this is true. In fact, it's by doing the complete opposite that these managers can become effective, high-performance leaders. When you look at a new situation, it's incredibly helpful to recognize the limitations of your own perspective and seek out those with different perspectives to gain better insight.

I took this lesson to heart upon my arrival at 20th Century Fox. The film division was very entrepreneurial at heart and being part of that group felt like being part of a family. That sense of family pulled at the heartstrings of its employees, and as a result, Fox employees tended to stay at the company for a long time. When I arrived, everywhere I turned there were people who had been at the company for decades and knew the organization and its culture far better than I. So, rather than come in with guns blazing, I thought it wise to learn and understand the Fox way of doing things. Here I was, arriving with my Disney perspective, but it was just as important, if not more so, to understand the Fox perspective.

It was the best decision I could have made. I learned so many things through the Fox lens that the Disney lens had filtered out. From the relationships with filmmakers to the mindset around spending levels; from the retail relationships around the DVD business to the analysis of contribution by division, the Fox approach was different. I shared my perspectives and listened to those of others, and as a company we made better decisions. As a result of our better decisions, we dominated the DVD business and sustained the highest overall margins in the industry. Sharing our perspectives and having a healthy debate around the options made us better.

Authentic leaders know their limitations and are proactive in getting fresh input from the people around them. Only then can they get the information and perspective they need to make the best decisions possible. It all starts with self-awareness.

Awareness, Perception, and Competence

The Conscious Competence theory, developed at Gordon Training International by Noel Burch in the 1970s, outlines four major shifts people make in their development, with the ultimate goal of becoming consciously competent. I believe that the world is now so complex that no one individual has the bandwidth to become consciously competent at everything, so it is essential to rely on the competence of others in order for any team to truly operate at high performance. As a leader, it is critical to see the connections between knowledge and awareness in order to understand how to benefit from the knowledge and skills of others:

1. "I know that I know" – *Consciously Competent*
2. "I know that I don't know" – *Consciously Incompetent*
3. "I don't know that I know" – *Unconsciously Competent*
4. "I don't know that I don't know" – *Unconsciously Incompetent*

For example, I know how to drive a car. I'm good at driving a car. That's a given. In this case, *I know that I know.*

Conversely, I don't know how to fly an airplane. I actually have no interest in flying an airplane. When I know I do not have the knowledge or skill for a particular task, I need to seek out someone who does. In this case, *I know that I don't know.*

Going to the next step, there are things *I don't know that I know*. An example of this from my personal life is that I apparently have always been a natural connector. I've been very successful at taking people from different ranges of behavior and finding constructive ways for them to work together. I guess you could say it's my purpose in life. I do it in my family, and I do it in departments and companies through my work. I've been able to get people to "play nice in the sandbox" together all of my life, but early on I *didn't know* this was a skill of mine until somebody pointed it out. It was a skill where I was unconsciously competent. It was, in fact, something that I didn't know that I knew.

My effectiveness as an authentic leader increased when I became *conscious* of this skill. I began to develop it more and deploy it strategically as I navigated difficult situations. It's the same for you. You have skills, talents, and abilities in which you may be unconsciously competent. Perhaps there's a blind area in your leadership that you *are unconsciously* developing. Feedback can play a great role in raising your level of awareness. Once you become aware of the skill, you can consciously work to further develop it.

Lastly, there are the things *I don't know that I don't know*. This is the area where leaders can get themselves into real trouble if they believe they are expected to have all the answers and solve all the problems without asking for help. In these situations, the leaders can shift into driving the business from a position of "I think I know (but I really don't)," which can be a very dangerous platform. Essentially, this level creates the illusion of certainty. When leaders spend time here, they tend to close themselves off to others' perspectives and only see things through their own biased lens. This frequently results in reaching improper conclusions and making bad business decisions.

Who Is Our Authentic Self?

There are so many questions out there about what it means to be authentic. Authenticity is not just blurting out whatever is on your mind; it has everything to do with how we *show up*. Do we show up at work each day professing to have all the answers, prescribing how our team should work moment to moment? Or do we show up as the best version of ourselves, having enough self-awareness to know that, particularly in today's disrupted world, we need the eyes and ears of our entire team to get a holistic view of the best way forward? Rather than coming from "I think I know," we are better to acknowledge that we don't know the answer. We just have to be genuine, honest, and authentic about the fact that we don't know everything.

When each of us is born, we start off as our Authentic Self, or True Self. We are honest, powerful, vulnerable, caring, loving, open, trusting, courageous, curious, etc. Then, something happens – LIFE. We experience events that cause us to form beliefs about the world, and those beliefs become our reality. Over time, our fixed beliefs and fixed behaviors begin to drive the substantial majority of our actions. It is all about stimulus-response. We experience something, our fixed beliefs interpret it and conform it to our reality, and then we respond with our programmed fixed behaviors.

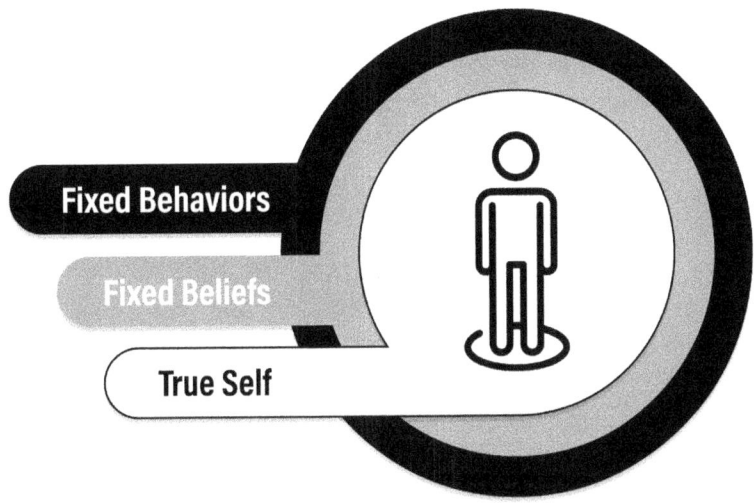

For example, imagine I am a caveman (I know, it's a bit far-fetched!). Imagine I have never seen fire or lightning. Then, one day, I am walking through the forest and lightning strikes a tree and it bursts into flames. This is a mystery to me. The next day, I am walking through the forest, and I see a burning tree. What do I conclude? That the tree was struck by lightning? Is that true? Maybe, maybe not. It may only be an illusion of certainty. This is why we need to be at least 1% open to the possibility that we may not be seeing things as they truly are.

If only we could disconnect from our automatic behavior, tap into our true selves, and STOP-LOOK-CHOOSE: stop the auto-response and see what is truly in front of us; look at the options available while considering input from others, and make a clear choice. We can break through—or interrupt—our fixed beliefs and fixed behaviors, stop operating with programmed responses, and instead respond authentically from our True Self.

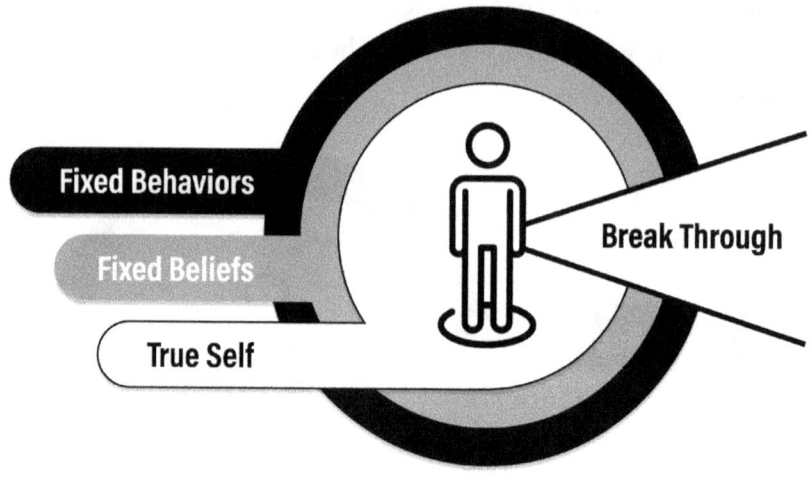

Owning Your Personal Power

In one of the Hallett Leadership ALP programs, we had a participant, whom I will call Brittany, from a strategy division. During the program orientation, Brittany immediately stood out. As in all the orientations, I asked the training cohort to share information about themselves in response to a prompt, as part of a path to build team unity in the group. In this case, the prompt was "Share a moment in your life when you experienced a high level of fear." In these exercises, I get a glimpse into just how open each participant is willing to be. Brittany was one of the first to speak, and she shared the fear she was experiencing due to some unique family circumstances. She was emotional, and conveyed the level of fear she had every day wondering whether her family would be OK. It was deep and authentic, and everyone in the room witnessed the personal power Brittany possessed. By personal power, I am referring to Brittany's ability to connect with people authentically and influence them constructively. There was no doubt Brittany possessed these traits.

Over the course of the ALP program, however, I realized that Brittany did not yet fully realize or embrace her personal power. As I had frequently done early in my career, Brittany tended to surrender her power to others and not stand up for herself. When others acted aggressively, Brittany often gave in or held back. She reached out to me to express her frustrations over some co-workers' behaviors that would belittle or take advantage of her. Brittany told me she was going to quit. She was going to leave the company.

I remember this like it was yesterday, maybe because I could see so much of myself in her. I remember all too well how easily I gave my power away to others in the early years of my life and career. Brittany believed that her vulnerability was a weakness when in reality, if conveyed authentically, vulnerability can be an incredibly powerful tool.

I instinctively coached Brittany and gave her feedback. I listened and coached her on constructive ways to improve each situation and related interactions. I urged her to trust herself and start listening to her own instincts… to learn how best to articulate them to others and identify opportunities to influence others rather than allowing others to manage how she feels. I said, "Don't you dare leave! Why would you let someone have that kind of power and influence over you? You are a star and you have so much to offer. You have so many gifts. You are smart, driven, powerful, and truly want what is best for the organization and its people. Find a way to be "at cause," rather than "at effect" of others. Stand up for who you are and show them the value of your contribution. Then, once they see what you have to offer, if you still want to leave, fine. But then you will be leaving on your terms, not theirs."

Brittany agreed. Over the next few months, she leaned into her personal power, willing to show up authentically regardless of the outcome. She found new ways to work with people in the group, and more broadly in the overall department. She collaborated with others, offering insights on how to improve strategies and the processes necessary to bring them to life. She stood up for herself and proudly embraced who she was and whatever ideas she had to share. Brittany had jumped into owning her personal power with both feet, and people could feel the difference.

At the end of the ALP program, Brittany participated in a small group presentation to a senior executive audience, including the company chairman, pointing out where the company was missing important strategic opportunities.

Brittany's presentation was so compelling that the company immediately shifted gears and pursued some of the strategies she recommended. The presentation was so impactful that suddenly, Brittany was a hot commodity, being vied for by various divisions in the organization… and even outside the company. In the end, Brittany did leave for another opportunity – but she left on her own terms.

How to *show up* authentically and own your own personal power are key pillars in Hallett Leadership's ALP program.

Companies don't lose many ALP graduates because the investment in the people typically increases their loyalty to the organization. And even though Brittany moved on, she left an indelible mark on the company!

The Power of Authenticity

In his article "Authentic Leadership: What It Is & Why It's Important," Matt Gavin makes reference to research outlined in the *Harvard Business Review* that indicates that most employees identify several positive impacts from authenticity in the workplace, including:

- **Better relationships with colleagues**
- **Higher levels of trust**

- **Greater productivity**
- **A more positive working environment**[5]

Investing the time and resources to develop authentic leadership in your organization can be of immense value and have a long-lasting impact on you, your people, and your company.

---

[5] Matt Gavin, "Authentic Leadership: What It Is & Why It's Important." Business Insights - Blog. Harvard Business School – Online, December 10, 2019. https://online.hbs.edu/blog/post/authentic-leadership?

Leadership Close Encounter - Kissing the Ring

Overseeing a finance division is always a bit of a balancing act. On the one hand, it is important for Finance to be a business partner to the group. On the other hand, Finance must keep tabs on budgets and exert influence to keep spending in line.

On one occasion, someone on my Finance team exerted their influence on a project that was very close to the chairman. The chairman, with whom I had worked for nearly ten years, picked up the phone and called me, stating that this time Finance had gone too far, and then hung up the phone.

Over the course of the next week, I reached out to the chairman – I emailed him and left messages with his assistant and voicemails on his cell phone but received no response.

I was scheduled for vacation the following week, so I sent one last email message. I reminded him that he knew me well enough to know that I always had the company's best interests at heart, and that he had known me long enough to give me the benefit of the doubt. I added that I was leaving on vacation, and I really didn't want to leave for my trip on these terms.

Literally one minute later, my phone rang. It was the chairman.

"Dean, buddy, how are you doing? Where are you going on vacation?"

We then discussed the situation, and he acknowledged in so many words that he understood where I was coming from and that I was only doing my job. And our relationship was completely back on track.

In his own way, he had only wanted me to seek his forgiveness – to kiss the ring! While I don't agree with his approach to the situation, I was happy to set my ego aside for the good of the team.

Give Feedback to Go Forward

Although feedback and open dialog are so important, many companies don't have a healthy structure for giving and receiving feedback. If we don't have a structure for it, we tend not to do it because of our concerns about whether or not we're going to hurt somebody's feelings.

To encourage feedback, I do structured exercises with my team. I usually can tell the right time for these exercises because there seems to be a revolving door into my office with people complaining about what others are doing or not doing. This revolving door informs me that the team has unspoken communication, and I can sense the level of frustration.

To kick things off, I walk into my staff meeting and say, "OK, today we're going to do something different." I literally have my team mingle with each other in the room and answer questions one-on-one, in a standing dyad.

For example, I might have them say, "What I admire about you as a leader is…" and then fill in the blank. Then I would have them say, "What I believe would make you a better leader is…" and they would give feedback.

Inevitably, when I do these types of exercises, people come up to me afterward and say, "You know, that was really uncomfortable," or, "I love when we do that." Whatever response the individuals have, it is nearly always unanimous that they feel it was helpful because people had an established structure, a mechanism for communicating feedback and expressing things they were unwilling to say before. I gave them a healthy way to deliver and receive feedback in a manner that demonstrated mutual trust and respect, and my team grew as a result.

I have found that giving and receiving honest feedback starts to knock down the walls that divide people inside of organizations. Feedback fosters awareness and authentic behavior, increases open communication and collaboration, and is very constructive in developing new ideas. It also creates a connection between people and brings the team closer together. As a result of those dynamics, people end up being more authentic in their interaction. Being more authentic leads to more engagement, interest, and excitement around the vision you're working towards. Teams become more creative and innovative, which drives better results.

Managers who are self-aware increase their level of authenticity as a leader. As managers begin to shift their beliefs about their need to be all-knowing and become more aware of their own levels of competence, as well as the competencies of their team, organizations begin to experience positive change. Collaboration transpires organically, teamwork thrives, and innovation kicks into high gear.

The culture becomes more open, trusting, and vulnerable. No longer are managers afraid to fail or ask for help. They actively seek out new perspectives, thoughts, and ideas. The key step is to get managers to be authentic and acknowledge they don't have all the answers, and to open the door for their teams to offer additional perspectives in order to have a bigger, better, and more complete understanding.

Chapter 3

Alignment

"The task of leadership is to create an alignment of strengths so strong that it makes the system's weaknesses irrelevant."
— Peter F. Drucker

"Building a visionary company requires one percent vision and 99 percent alignment."
— Jim Collins

"Alignment reflects an active ownership on the part of team members, not simply the absence of disagreement."
— Fred Smith

Seeing the challenges coming at us, and having no personal experience in supply chains, I approached my Studio CIO, who had been immersed in the Home Entertainment division during the exponential growth of the DVD business and had been deeply involved in developing Fox's direct-to-retail supply chain that serviced the likes of Walmart, Best Buy, and Target. As category managers for those retailers, Fox constantly developed new technology applications to provide the best data on our category, and my Studio CIO was at the center of it. He was the most business-minded IT leader I ever worked with. I knew his experience would be invaluable, and I needed to surround myself with experts who understood the aspects of the project that I did not.

Together, we worked on a game plan to move the Fox Media Framework forward. We agreed we wanted the best solution possible, and the only way to have that was to include stakeholders from every division. I went ahead and reached out to those I thought would be the best representatives, including people from Sales and Distribution, Operations, Engineering, IT, and Finance, and brought them all together.

We included high-level operational people from Theatrical, Home Entertainment, Television Distribution, and our backlot Technical Services group, who participated in developing and distributing some of the media as part of the physical supply chain. Everybody had to be involved in figuring out the system and what the corresponding processes needed to be.

Key stakeholders in this group became our task force for brainstorming the best way forward. All of these people would have some stake in how we would develop the Fox Media Framework. If the person I recruited to represent an area wasn't the head of their department or division, I made certain to loop in the head of that group as well. I was completely transparent so that all of the decision makers would know what we were doing.

Knowing we were looking to change a significant paradigm, the Studio CIO and I agreed that we should start with a vision, and that turned out to be the smartest thing we ever did.

We started the vision process by laying down some guiding principles on how we would move forward. All we focused on initially was what we thought would be the ideal outcome. In our very first session with the stakeholders, we came up with one specific guiding principle that received overwhelming unanimous support, and that principle became the foundation for the project's vision.

ALIGNMENT

This principle focused on the ideal result that we wanted to achieve: we would create a master digital version for each piece of intellectual property—be it a movie, television episode, or some other form of content—only once. That would drive the greatest efficiency because that single master version could then be used by all of the downstream distribution platforms.

If we could get people to agree that we should only make and master elements one time, then nobody could ever go back and say they should have their own supply chain. If you're going to make it only once, there could only be one supply chain; it would have to be integrated.

Not only did that enable us to create alignment within the group around the nature of what we wanted to build, but it also kept the hottest issue off the table – what group or entity would eventually own and control the Fox Media Framework. For now, we were only focused on the collective goal.

Our vision was simple and straightforward, but the actual mastering process was incredibly complex. Without getting too technical, all of the third-party distribution platforms around the world had different requirements, from technical display formats to bit rates to content protection protocols. Many of the platforms — from physical DVD to Apple to Comcast to Sky Broadcasting—had their own proprietary display specifications. We also had to contend with dubbing movies and television episodes into foreign languages and formatting television episodes to accept commercials of variable length.

We had to format our film and television masters in such a way that they could be used to accommodate all these variations. If we only wanted to create one content master, we would have to create it in a very high resolution and with enough flexibility that we could use it to derive every necessary downstream version.

So, our vision was extremely bold. Thankfully, we included representatives from each of our divisions on the task force, and every one of them engaged in the process and provided input. As a result, everyone aligned around the vision. Everybody agreed and said, "Absolutely, we should only be making one content master." In that moment, we were truly aligned. But alignment can be fleeting...

We still needed to operationalize the group and determine what changes would be necessary to make our vision a reality. There were many little things to be worked out, but we at least established the vision up front that said we wanted to make it once and then use it everywhere.

Once everybody was aligned around that vision, it was much simpler to resolve differences as they came up. With a clearly understood vision, it became difficult for any representative of any group to say, "We should do this on our own. We should have our own supply chain." That said, I'm not going to tell you no one ever uttered those words; there certainly were conflicts.

We had all kinds of issues to work through, and because I didn't have a stated mandate from the chairman confirming that I was the final decision maker, I was constantly having to influence the division presidents and department heads through the art of persuasion, as best I could. I knew there was no way we should allow the various divisions to build out multiple supply chains; it just didn't make sense. But I had to continually and repeatedly convince them of that. Creating alignment is an ongoing exercise, not a one-time deal.

It would have been much easier for me if I had the mandate validating my authority tucked away in my back pocket, but I didn't. I had asked to take leadership of the project, and my request had been granted. The chairman had given me the OK to lead the group and to lead the charge, but I didn't really have the final authority — not stated authority anyway.

Many times, I felt like I was out there on my own, or more accurately, the project leadership was on its own. We were responsible for casting the vision and influencing the division presidents and department heads to make the *project happen. I knew without the mandate the project was going to take longer than it would have otherwise.*

As I mentioned earlier, after decades of each division controlling every aspect of their operation, it was only natural for people to be territorial. I knew there were people in the divisions who were just not on board with establishing a single supply chain, and at times it felt like our efforts were being undermined. We had the Home Entertainment group, the TV Distribution group, and the backlot Technical Services group — groups that had worked independently for a very long time. There were hundreds of people involved in this process, either directly or tangentially, and many of them didn't want this change to happen.

Internal alignment around our vision, across the Enterprise Operations leadership team, held us together. We did go through several delays where we had to continually realign the team to overcome multiple challenges — but that was to be expected. A project of this magnitude and this much change was not going to sail through easily. And, luckily, we did gain at least some benefit from the delays because over the longer timeline we were able to take advantage of further technology advances in the digital world.

Mandate or no mandate, having a common vision around which everyone could align was essential to the success of the project.

Bullying is an open topic in today's world, but it wasn't when I was growing up, and it was too close to home. In fact, it was *in* my home. Michael, the boy next door, thought it was funny to have my older brother Kirk hit me. Whenever Michael said, "Permission granted," Kirk would begin hitting me, and then ironically the command "Hit Dean" meant he should stop. Our family moved when I was five, but the die was cast. Kirk continued the behavior for over a dozen years, though he no longer needed the commands "Permission granted" and "Hit Dean." It took its toll.

I remember being an extrovert in second grade, but that changed over time. I formed certain beliefs about myself, such as "It is better to be seen and not heard," and "My opinions don't matter," or more accurately, "I don't matter." I remember when I was 14, Kirk drove up to the house one day and jumped out of his car. He had broken his arm in a dirt bike crash and was sporting a cast. He ran towards me, swinging the cast violently, but luckily, I was faster and able to get away before he could land a blow.

On yet another occasion, I remember not following Kirk's instructions, so he grabbed an antique, decorative sword from my wall, put it to my throat, and told me he would kill me if I didn't do as he ordered. Needless to say, I was living in a constant state of fear.

Two Types of Leadership

Some business leaders operate the same way – instilling fear consciously or unconsciously so that employees don't feel the freedom to speak up. Rather than working with their teams to develop a vision that the entire organization can rally and align behind, these leaders operate under a command-and-control philosophy, and bite people's heads off.

The reality is that all leaders leave a wake, but some of these fear-instilling leaders are completely unconscious of the wake they leave and the impact they have on people's lives. These command-and-control type leaders use fear the same way a bully does to get people to do what they want. It's a horrible way to lead and an even worse way to live.

That's why I teach the organizations I work with the importance of leadership through *alignment*. Having an aligned organization creates more clarity, efficiency, and yes, even profitability.

Just think: *What if all your people were thrilled to come in to work each day, driven by a sense of purpose and esprit de corps? What if different divisions of your company proactively collaborated and communicated with each other? How would your organization's performance in the marketplace improve if it attracted the best talent in the industry?*

Alignment Is the Key to Your Management Development Plan

The lesson here is that *alignment* is the key. It's the cornerstone of any truly effective management development plan. *Alignment* can be defined as 100% willingness and commitment among all team members to pursue a shared vision. You want clear *alignment* around your goals and priorities, as well as the type of culture you desire and want to create. Coming into *alignment* unfolds in three parts:

1. Engaging everyone on the team by bringing them to the table and getting their input on company direction. This can even start at the division or department level.
2. Articulating a shared vision using tools for effective communication and collaboration.
3. Sustaining the use of these tools in order to maintain alignment as the group begins executing the shared vision.

When Your Company Is NOT in Alignment

An organization that is not in *alignment* can be modeled by the diagram below.

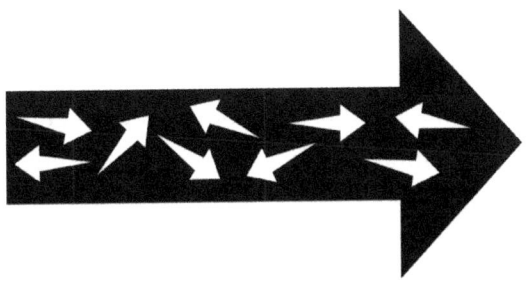

Overall, the company has a direction it desires to move in, represented by the large black arrow that encapsulates all the little white arrows.

This overarching direction is usually clear-cut and includes things like:

- Increased profits
- Marketplace dominance
- Competitiveness, retention, and innovation

The small white arrows inside of the black arrow represent different departments, or if the company is small, they can represent individual employees.

In the diagram above, the white arrows are all pointing in different directions. Each arrow has its own opinion, priority, and agenda. In other words, while each individual entity is participating in the overall left-to-right trajectory of the company as a whole, the priority of each arrow is pointing in its own direction, which, of course, may also be at odds with the directions of the others.

This simple diagram succinctly illustrates what it looks like when individual employees—or entire departments in larger organizations—place their own goals, priorities, and well-being above those of the overall company.

The Cost of Being Out of Alignment

Each individual vector, whether a person or department, moving in its own direction generates enormous friction. Time, energy, and capital are lost. Even company morale is diminished if you evaluate the organization from the perspective of HR.

Generally speaking, unaligned organizations are burning up energy through the friction caused by everyone operating under their own priorities. Just think about all the wasted resources and energy used when you spend all your time fighting battles within your own organization rather than using that time and energy to effectively present a united front against your competition.

Agreement vs. Alignment

The most common intervention used to treat an organization that is *out of alignment* is to force *agreement*. Yet, all *agreement* really means is that you make the little white arrows inside the big arrow merge into a single white arrow pointed in the direction that leadership insists they go.

This type of leadership is known as "command and control." Leaders throughout history have implemented it successfully, though it often results in a fear-based culture. It shows up in major public corporations just as it did in the armies of Frederick the Great from Prussia and Genghis Khan from Mongolia. But this is hardly *alignment*. If leadership can articulate a vision and implement it top-down through fastidious management and mandates, it is possible to score significant victories. This is the default leadership paradigm for most organizational cultures, so almost everyone is accustomed to it.

Most of us, if not all, know very well what it is like to be told what to do. Likewise, most people can affirm that being told what to do is not their favorite thing in the world. So, is this really the kind of organization you want? While *agreement* may get results, the employee who experiences such a leadership culture may not willingly follow or want to continue their work there. After all, there is typically little or no room in the *agreement* culture for personal growth and learning. As a result, retaining employees can be an issue.

Potential Impact of Agreement-Only Strategy

While *agreement* can lead to resounding wins, it leaves out the voices of the rank and file. When people aren't extended an opportunity to share their perspectives, opinions, and ideas, they may follow you (that is, "agree"), but they won't be fully invested like they are when they're aligned. Without this investment, you run the risk of your people becoming passive, sticking to their lanes, and refraining from speaking up when they notice something amiss.

When managers move higher up in a company, they often fear asking for help. They think they'll come off as weak or inadequate. As a result, they unintentionally create a culture of *agreement* or command and control. They lead by fear and threat rather than trust and authenticity. That's why establishing organizational *alignment* is such a foundational piece of high-performance leadership.

Employees in an organization operating under an *agreement* culture may not personally care one way or the other about what happens to the company. Sometimes, employees may even sit back and wait passively for the mandated direction to fail.

According to a Gallup poll, approximately 18% of the workforce is "actively disengaged," or actively aiming to subvert their employer's progress.[6] While *agreement* can lead to quick results, it may not be the best long-term strategy for success.

An *agreement* culture incentivizes the team to prescribe instructions, take orders, and maintain the status quo; to do something "because it's always been done that way."

Because It's Always Been Done That Way

There is a story, which may be a myth, about an experimenter who put five monkeys in a large cage. High up at the top of the cage, well beyond the reach of the monkeys, he placed a banana. Underneath the banana was a ladder.

The monkeys immediately spotted the banana, and one began to climb the ladder. As he did so, however, the experimenter sprayed him with a stream of cold water. Then, he proceeded to spray each of the other monkeys.

The monkey on the ladder scrambled off, and all five sat for a time on the floor, wet, cold, and bewildered. Soon, though, the temptation of the banana was too great, and another monkey began to climb the ladder. Again, the experimenter sprayed the ambitious monkey with cold water, and all the other monkeys as well. When a third monkey tried to climb the ladder, the other monkeys, wanting to avoid the cold spray, pulled him off the ladder and beat him.

Then, the experimenter removed one monkey and introduced a new monkey into the cage. Spotting the banana, he naively began to climb the ladder. The other monkeys pulled him off and beat him.

---

6 Harter, Jim, "Dismal Employee Engagement Is a Sign of Global Mismanagement." Gallup.com. Gallup, August 5, 2021. https://www.gallup.com/workplace/231668/dismal-employee-engagement-sign-global-mismanagement.aspx.

Here's where it got interesting. The experimenter removed a second one of the original monkeys from the cage and replaced him with a new monkey. Again, the new monkey began to climb the ladder and, again, the other monkeys pulled him off and beat him – including the monkey who had never been sprayed.

By the end of the experiment, none of the original monkeys were left and yet, despite none of them ever experiencing the cold, wet spray, they had all learned never to try and go for the bananas.

And if you were to ask one of the monkeys why they beat the monkey who ascended the ladder, they might just say, "Because it's always been done that way."

Achieving True Alignment

Now that we have explored what alignment *is not*, let's explore the best model we currently have for what it *is*. The diagram below shares elements in common with the previous two.

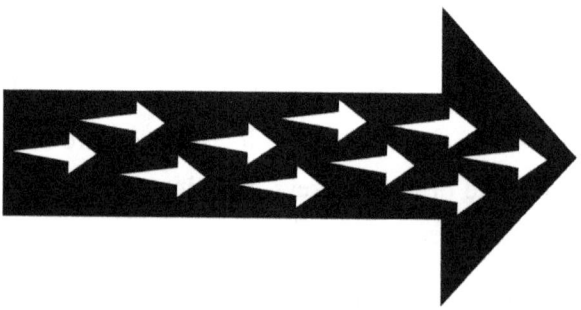

Like the *out of alignment* organization, the larger black arrow is full of individual entities, departments, or people. Like the organization in *agreement*, they are all pointing in the same direction. The difference here is that the individual entities have remained independent agents. They are moving together *as one*, but they have not *become one*.

This is very important. Unlike the folks at the *agreement* strategy company, no one has forced anyone to do anything. The individual arrows are moving of their own volition and in the direction they helped establish, which happens to be the same direction as everyone else. There is no active disengagement here; in fact, it is the opposite. The little arrows may even be fired up to appear in the workplace every morning, taking on their projects in a collaborative and interdependent manner.

An Eleventh-Hour Rally

At the end of the ALP Program, small groups of four or five people research and present to senior management on key issues facing the company and/or the industry. In one program, the members of one of the project groups were, for various reasons, having significant difficulties working with each other. The group members had developed a lack of trust for each other – something that had been going on for several weeks.

In ALP, we work on our leadership skills all the way through the program, participating in Discovery Model exercises, including giving and receiving feedback. While the training is essential, the real test comes when participants integrate their learnings into their ongoing daily activities. One of the many benefits of the ALP project presentations is that they provide an opportunity to incorporate the program learnings into a real business activity. Many a time I have seen groups wait until the final presentations to break through their own resistance and come together as a team. I always say: every group is different, but every group ultimately *gets there*.

It was about one week before this group's final presentation date, and two or three team members were literally not even talking to each other. One of those team members invited me for coffee just to talk, and she said to me, "You know, it's really unfortunate that the program has to end this way."

I looked at her and said, *"Really? The last time I checked, the program wasn't over yet.* I don't know about you, but if it were me, I wouldn't let it end this way. I'd call this group together, get in a room, and do whatever it takes to get through our issues with each other, so that when we get on that stage and present to senior management, we have each other's backs. We are a solid, single force doing this project together, working together."

She replied, "You know what? You're right."

So, she pulled the group together, got them all in a room, and closed the door. She essentially wasn't going to let anybody leave until everything that needed to be said was said. Everybody communicated what they had been holding back, and they cleared the air. I understand it was somewhat cathartic, but incredibly constructive. They realized that they didn't need to be the best of friends after the program – but for purposes of this exercise and presenting this project to senior management, they had to be one unit. They had to be aligned in principle, in approach, and in action. And most importantly, they had to have each other's backs.

They worked through their issues… and to be honest, they were one of the groups going into the presentations that I was most worried about… about how well they were going to present.

And… they knocked it out of the park.

So, just because you may not be friends with someone, or agree with someone, doesn't mean that you can't connect with them, get aligned, and create a positive impact with them inside the company.

From a high-performance leadership perspective, overcoming conflict at work can look like setting aside the expectation of personal friendship, and instead aligning around a shared vision and common goal.

Alignment Unites the Team

According to Alessandra Gyben, Marketing Director at GreenRope, "Organizational alignment is the key to any successful organization… In today's digital environment, it is more important than ever to deliver streamlined and personalized customer experiences. The only way to truly accomplish this is through organizational alignment."[7] Gyben goes on to say that true organizational alignment is when the entire enterprise team, without exception, shares a common vision for the organization.

Gyben indicates that siloed organizations have departments working with disparate, incomplete information over the course of product lifecycles, and do not share their information with other departments. This approach may allow one or two departments to thrive, but they do so at the expense of the overall organization.

Gyben further cites a Clear Company survey that reports that 97% of employees and executives believe lack of alignment within a team impacts the outcome of a task or project, and 86% of employees and executives cite lack of collaboration or ineffective communication for workplace failures.

The results are staggering!!

---

7   Gyben, Alessandra, "The Importance of ORGANIZATIONAL Alignment and How to Achieve It." MarTech Advisor, April 25, 2019. https://www.martechadvisor.com/articles/digital-transformation/the-importance-of-organizational-alignment-and-how-to-achieve-it/.

Leadership Close Encounter – The Music Doesn't Match the Words

There was so much positive energy at Fox when I arrived, and so many great people. There was an entrepreneurial energy at the studio, and people were mostly excited to be working with each other.

Our chairmen were very hands-on. Even though we didn't have a formal Franchise Management group early on, our chairmen worked diligently to ensure that we coordinated the efforts of our divisions, and that we had continuity in our marketing messages around the world.

One of our senior executives was not a fan of the level of chairman involvement and resisted what he perceived as prescriptive leadership. He never shared this with me directly. He didn't have to. I could see in his face and in his actions that he was not aligned with the overall organizational vision, and that he preferred to work to his own rhythm, in his own tempo. Over time, this executive decided it took too much energy to argue for his strategy and position, and instead took on a passive-aggressive demeanor.

He developed the habit of nodding his head in agreement with the chairmen even though he had no intention of complying. I repeatedly watched as he agreed with them, only to then leave the room and put his own strategy in place in his division. It ultimately reached a point where there was no effective dialog or healthy debate at all.

Whether I agree with the level of involvement of my superiors or not, I know one thing for sure: working without any alignment will not solve the problem.

Ultimately, our chairmen realized we needed to make changes in this division in order to develop a healthy level of dialog and collaboration.

ALIGNMENT

How Do You Get to Alignment?

The way is simple. If you desire to get all the little arrows inside of your organization moving enthusiastically together in the same direction, *it is time to talk*. What do I mean?

You can start by creating an environment of openness. Bring your people to the table and invite them into a conversation about the organization. Get them talking about work, sharing ideas with each other, and discussing the challenges each of them is facing. Invite them to suggest solutions of their own and generate ideas for processes that facilitate collaboration. Whatever you decide to discuss, or what or how to change, just get people talking. Once they begin to open up and trust each other, they are walking the road to *alignment*.

By soliciting input and inviting your people to the table as active participants in the creation of a common vision and strategy, you can transform them into committed stakeholders. They then have emotional and intellectual "skin in the game" as to how the company fares after undertaking the shared vision.

Establish Alignment on Internal Priorities Before External Priorities

Many organizations have a vision statement of some kind. These tend to refer to service goals and market performance. While these are incredibly valuable, I would propose that before creating any kind of vision statement that proclaims an organization's intentions for the outside world, the first thing you should do is establish a vision for a desired culture *inside your organization.* In order to achieve buy-in and alignment around this vision, I suggest the organization develop an inclusive process involving all of its people, or at least an adequate representation of those decision makers.

Alignment Begins with Trust

It's essential to foster an environment of openness and trust in order to support your people in getting aligned. With an open and trusting environment in place, it is then time to move on to an inclusive conversation that increases alignment among everyone on the team. There are tools and mental frameworks that can support you in the process of building trust and coming into alignment. Some of these tools revolve around healthy communication, giving and receiving feedback, and clearing the air of obstacles and misunderstandings.

It is also important to engage with Discovery Model exercises and low-risk activities where participants can experiment and begin to experience collaboration in order to understand that the team members are better together than they are alone. When you build trust among the people who sustain the work, you'll be well positioned for moonshots, innovation, and creativity of every kind. If I told you that each individual within your organization has potentially infinite reserves of thought and creativity, what would that mean for your organization as a whole? There is no limit to the shared imagination and thought of your entire organization.

The Case for Alignment Sells Itself

Alignment is the key to your team's development plan. As if the prospects of creativity, innovation, and increased performance weren't enough, in an aligned culture, many participants report enhanced meaning and satisfaction in their overall lives by collaborating with others to realize something larger than one's individual paycheck.

Alignment requires a shared vision. The vision I share as a placeholder vision for each organization that trains with Hallett Leadership is ***"To create an open and collaborative culture where creativity and innovation thrive."***

I have found this placeholder vision to be a great framework for coming into true alignment. With alignment, you too can come to the same conclusion that Walt Disney did when he said, "My greatest reward is that I have been able to build this wonderful organization."

Chapter 4

Building the Best Teams

"Build for your team a feeling of oneness, of dependence on one another, and of strength to be derived by unity."
— Vince Lombardi

"The strength of the team is each individual member. The strength of each member is the team."
— Phil Jackson

"To build a strong team, you must see someone else's strength as a complement to your weakness not a threat to your position or authority."
— Christine Caine

As with any organization, in order to establish the right culture, we needed to address all three aspects of the Enterprise Operations culture: 1) the people, 2) the organizational structure, and 3) the processes – but we had to start with #1, the people. To shift an organization into high performance, we needed to build the best team.

Now that we were looking to build and operationalize the Fox Media Framework, we needed more than a task force; we needed an operating group. To build this group or team, it seemed logical to solicit input from members of the task force. I separated the task force into three teams and asked each of them to spend some time pulling together a recommended organizational structure and workflow for Enterprise Operations.

Each team presented, and the proposals were incredibly consistent and aligned in their approach. The only substantial difference among them was in who they recommended to lead the new group. We all knew we needed to be sensitive to the needs of each Fox division, so it was no surprise that every team's recommendation suggested pulling in experienced personnel from each operating division.

I knew it would take a real team effort to get this new operating group established and functioning at peak performance, so it was critical to get the team aligned quickly. We were creating the new group by combining pre-existing teams from the various operating divisions, so we were essentially merging different cultures together. That meant we were likely to come across varying degrees of resistance to moving forward in our new direction. Rather than allowing this resistance to fester in each division's ranks for an extended period, we thought it best to rip off the Band-Aid and combine the groups immediately. So, we moved all of the supply chain and sales servicing teams under one organizational umbrella. Even though we physically weren't moving their chairs on Day One, we wanted to change their reporting line immediately, so we just flipped the switch. We essentially said, "You're now part of this group called Enterprise Operations." And in that moment, the new team absorbed the responsibility for all physical and digital media deliveries.

Flipping that switch had an added emotional charge related to headcount implications. Headcount at Fox was always precious, and no division wanted to give up existing seats to the new division. In order to build Enterprise Operations' momentum and not create unnecessary additional friction, we found some open headcount in other areas to ease the pain. But it was more than just the heads. So much of this was about the desire to control. Given the length of time each division had controlled all of its own processes, this desire for control was completely understood and anticipated, but nevertheless it was definitely going to be a rough start.

To create greater alignment, we pulled together the new Enterprise Operations team for a kickoff event. It was important for everyone to feel that they had a place in this new group, and that they had the support of senior leadership to build something great. We invited the group to participate in some Leadership and High-Performance workshops to build deeper levels of mutual trust and respect that would be essential to establishing a process of continual improvement for the Fox Media Framework.

While our vision was to generate only one master element for each piece of content, we knew we weren't going to get there overnight. We needed to try new things as a group, support each other, listen to varied perspectives, and be willing to fail and learn from our mistakes. We needed the team to be accountable and responsible for each other — to have each other's back, and to trust each other. There was no room for blame here. Without such an approach, we would limit our own creativity and innovation.

As we expected, once the team was in place, we were met with a multitude of challenges that stood in the way of building our desired culture.

We had tapped the head of the Home Entertainment physical supply chain to run the Fox Media Framework. There were strong external perceptions that because this leader had come from the Home Entertainment physical side of the business, he would favor the Home Entertainment business in decisions around building the digital supply chain and determining operational priorities.

One thing I learned when I led Disney Shared Services was that it is impossible to overcommunicate. No matter how many times I believed we had conveyed messages, it was never enough. It's similar to my comments about various Fox division leaders falling out of alignment on the digital supply chain week after week. Good communication was imperative.

So, with our new Enterprise Operations leader in place, I was crystal-clear that in order to demonstrate there was no inherent bias favoring Home Entertainment, we needed to be completely transparent and overcommunicate to the Theatrical and TV Distribution groups. We spent an enormous number of cycles communicating about every step we were taking.

Another challenge when we first formed Enterprise Operations was that some people in the operating divisions were quick to publicize any errors made by the new Enterprise Operations team. When something went wrong, these people were quick to suggest their point of view that Enterprise Operations was failing. The truth, however, was that Enterprise Operations had inherited the legacy processes that had been in place in each division for quite some time. Enterprise Operations inherited these existing systems and processes on the day we launched. The individual operating divisions had experienced the same errors and issues for years, but units outside their divisions had never heard about them. In the past, the operating divisions managed and resolved any such errors within their own walls. The new Enterprise Operations breakdowns were occurring solely as a result of the legacy processes that had been in place for years.

For example, one group used email chains as their order tracking system, so when a customer wanted to know the status of their order, it was nearly impossible to determine. And just as bad, there was no way to build an order status report in real time. These were not shortcomings of the new Enterprise Operations group – we were just revealing challenges that had existed in the processes of the operating business units for years. Those operating groups, while the best in the industry at driving profitability, were not experts at supply chain. The challenges did not suddenly arise from the vision and *approach of the Fox Media Framework, but rather from the institutional processes and systems that Enterprise Operations inherited.*

And still another challenge we were living with was people who wanted to be viewed as being on board with the new direction, but who were still loyal to their individual operating divisions. These individuals would tell Enterprise Operations what we wanted to hear, and then communicate a vastly different message back to their division presidents. Time after time we would hear of their support for Enterprise Operations, stating that it was absolutely the way we needed to go, and then they would report back to their divisions that it was not the right solution, too many errors were being made, and that the divisions should take back their own supply chains. Without a public mandate, we spent countless hours repeatedly rehashing the same issues. It was definitely an efficiency killer in moving the project forward.

When seeking to align a team, my ideal approach is to keep everyone on the team. My approach for years with new visions and operational procedures had been to give people the benefit of the doubt and give them enough opportunity to shift their attitude and approach into alignment with the new way forward. Enterprise Operations was no exception.

To build the best team, we needed a team where everyone had each other's back. It never ceases to amaze me how much energy a detractor can drain from a team. We needed to move quickly and effectively, and we didn't have the time or the energy to carry dead weight, let alone those rowing the other way. So, while we gave everyone ample opportunity to come into alignment, those people who were unrelenting and continually looked to undermine the effort were eventually let go.

To build the best Enterprise Operations unit, we knew we also needed to look beyond the Enterprise Operations leadership. We needed to look at the leadership of other groups that would work in tandem with Enterprise Operations. Given the level of technology integration that would be part and parcel to the Enterprise Operations function, Information Technology (IT) was one such area.

A key IT decision we made early on for the digital supply chain was to have it run on the same network backbone as our other studio network traffic. We decided to route all of our digital media through the same network pipes as our other digital traffic. This was important because we wanted the linkage between our business applications and the Fox Media Framework to be solid; however, our regular network wasn't built to handle this load. Our legacy network backbone and data centers were dated and needed significant updating, and they needed it ASAP!

I was extremely lucky to have a stellar Studio CIO, and I knew he could grow as his role expanded. We worked together to address the network infrastructure that was buckling under the weight of the digital supply chain. We moved expeditiously to ensure the entire Fox Media Framework would not be compromised. At that same time, we also worked together to upgrade our IT leadership, data center, and cloud strategy – a strategy that was vital to the safety and security of storing and distributing all of our digital assets.

At the end of the day, we needed the best cross-divisional team. We needed high performance leaders at every level of the digital supply chain, with great trust and vision permeating the group. The risks associated with any other approach were far too great.

One afternoon, when our son Drew was around age 14, he came home and we started a discussion around his behavior. He didn't like the direction of the conversation, became frustrated, grumbled under his breath, and headed towards his room. I knew the discussion was not over, so I followed, and as I approached his room, he slammed the door in my face. I opened the door and said firmly, "Not in my house!" and I immediately began sobbing uncontrollably.

A bit of background: We had a teenage neighbor across the street who was always getting into trouble. He was high much of the time. He would actually be high while walking on the pitched, shingled roof of his parents' home. Our family watched him get arrested multiple times, including once as he was tackled by the police in his own front yard. The last time he was arrested, his parents sold the house and moved while he was incarcerated. As they were leaving, they told us, "We hope he never finds us. He has ruined our lives."

So, as I watched my son taking steps to shut out my wife Kelli and me, I instinctively knew I needed to somehow change the dynamic. The most important thing to me was keeping our family together, no matter what. So, even though it was not by conscious design, when I began sobbing uncontrollably, Drew stopped in his tracks. He had never seen me do that before, and with hindsight he clearly saw that my love for him was more important than anything else in that moment, including risking that I might be perceived as weak or imperfect. I was willing to be completely open and vulnerable with him.

We then sat for a while that afternoon and talked about what was bothering him. He danced around it, but I could clearly see that he felt lonely and isolated. I could see that he didn't feel like he fit in socially among his peers. At one point in the conversation, I told him that I understood how he felt, to which he retorted, "You have no idea how I feel."

And so, I replied... "I think I do know, and let me tell you why. When I see you in front of the house and there are ten, twelve, or fifteen of your friends hanging around talking, and you are on the periphery of the group just listening to what others have to say, but not contributing to the conversation, it isn't because you think what you have to say is unimportant. It is because your mind is blank, and you have absolutely no idea what to say."

Drew's jaw dropped, and he simply said, "How do you know that?"

I told him, "Because that was me when I was your age. I know exactly how you feel."

Drew and I had an amazing talk that afternoon. At age 14, most of his friends had physically outgrown him, and he got picked on. So, he was neither confident nor comfortable in his own skin. Now, maybe that is common for 14-year-olds, but that didn't mean we couldn't work to improve things. I reached out to my mentor, Jack, to see if he knew of a program Drew could attend to boost his confidence. Jack told me about Awakening the Warrior Within, a transformational self-defense program offered by Dawn Callan, CEO at Transformational Arts Institute. It was primarily a program for adults, but I contacted the organization, and they agreed that Drew could attend if I accompanied him.

Over the two-day program, participants received training on how to attack and make the first move if physically threatened with no way to escape. On the second day, two men, each about 6'5" clothed in soft body armor, attacked each program participant three times, each time under a different scenario. I was intimidated by these men, and I have to believe Drew was too; however, Drew embraced the training and went after these men using the techniques he had learned, and he was incredible. And when we returned home, Drew carried himself differently, and people could sense it. No one picked on him anymore, and he no longer stayed on the periphery of his circle of friends. He didn't tell them about the program, nor did he threaten anyone; they could just sense the change in his presence.

This was my family, and I was willing to do whatever it took to make my family great. I approach my teams in much the same way. I bring together the right people, invest in them, have them support each other to be their best, and have them realize that they are better together than they are alone.

Tips for Building the Best Teams

Building the best teams starts with defining a cultural vision from the top. As I mentioned earlier, at Hallett Leadership the placeholder vision we offer as a starting point for our clients is to have an open, collaborative culture where creativity and innovation thrive. Once we have that vision, we must address the most important element in achieving that vision: creating alignment, which we touched on in the last chapter. You can have the best people on board but if they are all moving independently, you will find it incredibly challenging to make progress.

Evolution of Natural Systems

Natural systems continually evolve in order to survive. As their environments change, natural systems must change as well. Organizations are no different. That is why so many companies today seek to implement processes of continual improvement. Often times an organization will have a vision that serves as a North Star, guiding the overall direction of the company. The ultimate vision may never be completely attained, but the vision can provide direction and focus to an organization in this complex world. Many companies today, in our volatile world, use their vision as a means of driving self-disruption within the organization. Their motivation is driven by the likelihood that someone is bound to disrupt their business model, and they would prefer to be proactive and drive that disruption themselves.

As reflected in the illustration below, when a new vision is embraced, there is a gap between the current condition and the vision. When setting out to achieve this vision, it is important to take inventory of the current condition in order to understand the nature of the gap. By asking ourselves, what do we need to KEEP, what do we need to DELETE, and what do we need to CREATE NEW, we can develop strategies to work toward our ultimate vision.

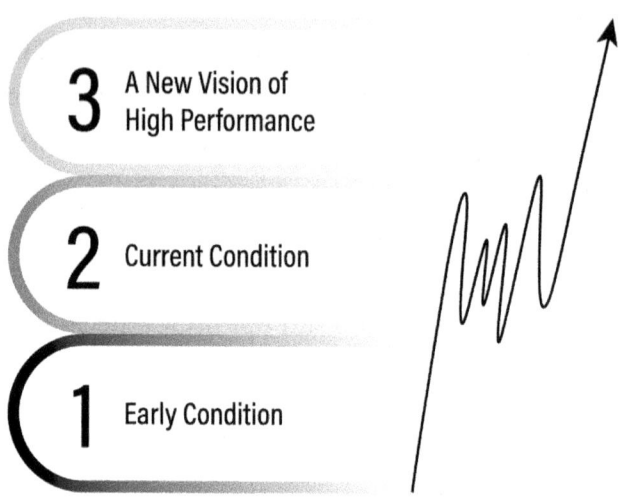

A Typical Romance

To better understand how this process works, let's look at the evolution of another natural system: a romantic relationship. Imagine two people meet and quickly form a strong connection. Early in the relationship, the energy is incredible. The two feel a sense of timelessness, joy, and well-being as they spend entire afternoons by the lake walking hand in hand. One sings and strums the guitar as the other listens. They laugh and fall into silent awe, letting the conversation meander in the most delightful ways.

Weeks and months go by, with time drawing out the best in each partner. The energy between them seems to be growing by the day, with no imaginable end in sight.

And then something happens…

The Energy Dissipates

Conflict and friction enter the scene. The couple feels a sense of irritation, and the two find themselves quarreling. Trust issues, based on past relationships, may have worked their way into the couple's interaction. Suddenly, the bliss, flow, timelessness, and unbounded generosity of spirit have given way. The energy dissipates and grows unstable, entering a state of entropy. The couple is lost for explanation as to how things could have changed so quickly.

Looking to restore the energy and feelings of the past, the two instinctively make attempts to repeat the activities that previously brought them so much joy and delight: the same dates, the same activities, the same thoughts, words, and deeds… but instead of harnessing the energy flow again, they can't seem to get any traction. The reality is, the relationship (or system) has evolved, and what worked in the past may no longer be what the relationship needs.

At this moment, the couple faces a choice – try to ignore what they are feeling and hope it goes away, attempt to recreate the past, or articulate a new vision that will provide a framework for them to engage as they move forward into a new, unknown reality.

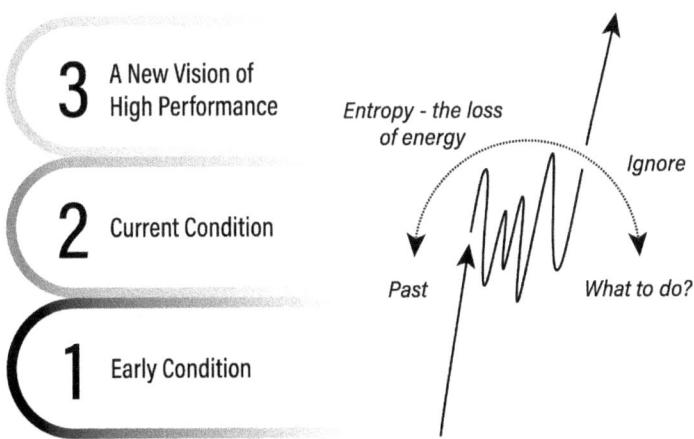

If they choose to ignore the situation or attempt to go back to the way it was, they will not address the real issues at hand, and will likely continue to lose energy in the relationship, and no longer grow together.

A New Trajectory – Returning to Growth

If, however, they choose to articulate a new vision, they will have something to aim for together. And to set out on that path, they can partner with each other to determine which elements in the relationship are working that they want to KEEP, which elements are not working that they want to DELETE, and which elements they want to CREATE NEW in order to add to the relationship. It is in this process that the couple can dig deep into their trust issues and together determine a new way forward, add energy to the relationship by entering a state of syntropy, and once again grow as a team.

Business Was Booming

The evolutionary path that companies follow can be similar to romantic relationships.

In 2001, the 20th Century Fox film studio began a period of incredible ascension. It was the first year of what became a string of eight record years – a period quite similar, in fact, to the ascension of the romantic relationship described above.

The studio at the time operated much like an Olympic relay team. Each high-performing division produced or distributed outstanding products or services, then handed the baton off to the next division in a linear sequence. Initially, Theatrical Production produced each film and passed it to Theatrical Marketing and Distribution. Once the film launched in theaters, Theatrical Marketing and Distribution passed the baton to Home Entertainment, which in turn passed it to TV Distribution. The company was operating on all cylinders not only with film launches, but also with the sale and licensing of library titles on DVD and international TV platforms. Everyone at the company was winning.

The company ran its businesses as well-oiled machines on a tightly orchestrated assembly line. Each division was great at making its area the best in the industry. Leadership within each division tended to the needs and prerogatives of its own business – which presented few challenges because the organization, people, and processes were arranged ideally for the existing marketplace.

Most notably, since business was booming, there was no compelling need to significantly alter the process. Little of the work produced in a single division impacted the perspectives or needs of the other divisions. The people of Fox took incredible pride in their work and the successful performance of their creative outputs in the marketplace.

Waking Up in a New, Volatile Marketplace – Entropy Enters the Scene

The release of *Avatar* in 2009 was the gem in the crown of the ascent Fox started in 2001. Profits on the film broke all-time records, company morale was high, and it seemed Fox was positioned to take on vistas no one could have imagined just a few short years before. However, at the peak of the growth, circumstances suddenly changed.

The year 2008 was one of incredible disruption, beginning with the commencement of the Great Recession. DVD piracy was rampant, affecting the entire marketplace. But that wasn't all. True video on demand (VOD) was also beginning to resonate. Consumers could now have movies and television shows delivered directly into their homes through an internet connection with the simple click of a button – and no amount of discount DVD bins at Walmart was going to change that.

In the DVD category alone, the entire film and television industry began to witness an ongoing decline in sales, with no indication that things would return to prior peak levels. The movie industry's old way of doing business was no longer as profitable.

A confluence of factors very quickly prompted Fox leadership to reassess the entire way it approached the business.

Creating Alignment to Overcome the Plateau

Like the couple who aligned around a shared new vision, Fox leadership knew there was no way of winning in the new marketplace following yesterday's playbook. The studio leadership knew it needed to align around a new vision.

Prior to the turbulence, each studio division was able to navigate its respective territory without concern over its impact on the other divisions. The growth in the business had been substantial in all areas, so there had been plenty of room for each business to grow. Moving forward, though, that was no longer going to be the case.

In order to drive profitability across the company as a whole, each division needed to further understand the impact of its actions on the other areas. This necessitated a change in the culture of the company. Moving forward, it would be critical to ensure that the organization, people, and processes were structured to foster a greater level of open, horizontal communication across the various vertical operating divisions. The vision for the company culture became a focal point for the future:

To create an open and collaborative culture where creativity and innovation thrive.

Leadership set out on a new path. It pulled senior management together, then held a town hall to communicate with the entire employee base. The message was clear – more than ever, the company needed to align around the vision and operate as a single unit.

Keep-Delete-Create New

As the Fox studio set out to pursue its new vision, we hosted workshops for all levels of employees, so that everyone would focus more on the impact to other divisions of their own division's decisions and approach. Middle manager training was a key focus because that group would play a key role in driving day-to-day collaboration across the enterprise, enabling each division to do its work with input and robust communication from all sides of the business.

The studio assessed what aspects of its culture were working that it wanted to KEEP, which approaches and mindsets it needed to DELETE, and what other elements it needed to CREATE NEW in order to ascend on its new syntropic growth trajectory.

Develop and Engage Your People

While creating alignment is the most important element in building the best teams, the second most important element is developing and engaging your employees. On the development side, this involves not just technical training, but even more importantly EQ and cultural training. This investment will not only improve the individuals, it will also increase their level of engagement and teach them how to think about the best decisions for the health of the entire company. It will increase their level of accountability for the overall company team and results, not just for their own individual area.

Training and developing your people increases and maintains a trust level across the team – a trust that can be threatened when you bring in someone from the outside. Sure, there are plenty of reasons to hire in someone new, from specific skillsets to a fresh perspective. Yet, it is important to remember that there are vast resources of untapped skills and ideas in your current team. And the investment you make in your current team will drive the level of trust, loyalty, and retention through the roof.

Other Team-Building Considerations

Once you establish organizational alignment around your vision, and train and develop your team, there are additional key steps that you can take to continue building and maintaining the best team:

- *Incentivize them by rewarding desired behavior.* It is important to structure incentives that align with the vision. It is very possible that both financial and non-financial incentives have been rewarding the team for behavior that is no longer aligned with the new vision. Rewarding bad behavior can lead the team to question the company's commitment to the new vision and can undermine everything.

- *Hire smart.* So often we look for the brightest mind when we recruit. Of course, we want high intellectual capital at our companies, but not at the expense of the company culture. Be sure to seek a great cultural fit. It takes time to build a great culture, but bringing in the wrong element can undo a lot of hard work in a flash. Remember, one bad apple can ruin the whole bunch.

- *Hire for your weakness.* We are better together than we are alone. We want diverse skills, talents, and perspectives on the team. So, if I am an inspirational CEO and my key strength is big ideas, I want to ensure my leadership team includes executives that are exceptional at execution. Or, if strategy is not my greatest strength, I want to surround myself with high-quality strategists that can help guide the business. At the end of the day, we want to be sure the team as a whole has all the requisite attributes to be successful.

Vulnerability Creates Connection Across the Team

In every Accelerated Leadership Program, we view Brené Brown's Ted Talk, "The Power of Vulnerability," in which Brené describes vulnerability as having the courage to show up even when we cannot control the outcome.

One such program included a young man whom we will call Steve, from the Fox Consumer Products division. Steve has a strong personality, along with a sarcastic wit (I know because I can have a sarcastic wit as well). During our program sessions, Steve would make a number of comments that created unease in the room.

In the ALP programs, we always work hard to create an environment where the participants can take ownership of the program and provide valuable feedback to push each other to be their best. However, Steve's strong personality kept the others at bay.

The participants would reach out to me to express their concerns, so I encouraged them to speak with Steve directly. Even after much encouragement, though, no one was taking that step. While we want ALP participants to take ownership, I am always asking myself what steps I can take to shift the group in the right direction and create program momentum. It is part of my own personal journey of continual improvement.

I never ask anyone in the program to do something I am not willing to do myself, so I decided to reach out to Steve and invite him to coffee. I wanted to get to know him better and understand what was driving his behavior, and he began to show a vulnerability I had not seen before.

Steve opened up to me about difficulties he was experiencing on the family front, which had been contributing to stress on the job. After Steve disclosed his situation to me, I shared with him the feelings others in the group had expressed, and as I suspected, he had not been aware. It isn't always easy to receive feedback, but to this man's credit, he listened and took it in. He reflected deeply on how his behavior was affecting the group, and how team members' perception of him could be affecting his own career and experience of the workplace.

Steve clearly did not want others to feel this way about him, and he agreed to turn things around. And so he did!

He returned to the group, and within a short period of time, Steve was like a man transformed. He tempered the sarcasm and side talk. Instead, he took to soliciting others' opinions and ideas, including everyone in the conversation, and generally supporting and collaborating with his teammates.

Steve made an effort to get to know everyone in the program at a deeper level and let them see the wholehearted side of him he had not previously shared. He connected deeply to the point where others felt a great deal of newfound trust with him, and he evolved into one of the more dynamic leaders in the cohort.

Within this short period, Steve became one of the most trusted and liked members of the group. People regularly came to him for his advice and input, or just to have a sounding board for problems they were working through.

Steve had not acquired some new strategic competency, nor had he deployed a new tactic... he simply let his guard down and began interacting with sincerity and compassion. And it transformed the entire team. It raised the team unity and alignment to a whole new level.

Look for opportunities to bring your teams together in a wholehearted, authentic way. It will develop deep connections and engage members of the team in profound new ways.

Camaraderie Promotes Group Loyalty and Dedication to Work

An article published by Teambuilding.com cites a *Harvard Business Review* article in which Christine M. Riordan mentions studies that explore how soldiers form close bonds because they "believe in the purpose of the mission, rely on each other, and share the good and the bad as a team." Teambuilding goes on to say, "As you can imagine, this camaraderie would be invaluable if transferred to the workplace." It further posits that one of the main objectives of team building is forging bonds among employees. When teams participate, the strengthened group loyalty and dedication to work result in increased productivity and engaged employees.[8]

---

8   Alexis, Michael, "Team Building Statistics & Facts " Teambuilding.com." teambuilding.com, July 15, 2021. https://teambuilding.com/blog/team-building-statistics.

Leadership Close Encounter – Rewarding Bad Behavior

There was a time in my career when I thought I was in the midst of an amazing organizational transformation. We had a new leader, and she wanted an open culture where all of the team's great ideas could be brought forward. Where we could have a healthy debate around diverse perspectives to arrive at the best solutions on how to build sustainable growth into the company. Where the people would feel empowered and engaged in the organization's vision. I believed we were on the brink of an incredible journey.

We communicated emphatically that we wanted a culture where openness and collaboration would be rewarded, and most of the team, even if not all, were thrilled.

The message around this transformation had tremendous traction. We engaged with our teams and had an onslaught of new ideas that worked their way through the organization to senior management. We formed task forces to work through and prioritize these ideas in order to capitalize most effectively on them.

And then it happened....

We went through a brief period where our products underperformed, and priorities suddenly shifted at the top. We needed our next few products to launch successfully, no matter what. We were working in a creative business, and some of the individuals who had been resisting the new collaborative approach leveraged this new predicament to their advantage. Knowing they were needed to get through this period, they pushed for—and received—promotions and expanded responsibilities, despite displaying behaviors that were contrary to the open, collaborative style we had said would be rewarded.

And that was all it took....

The leadership lost its integrity. After all the talk about the new way forward, the actions said loudly that nothing had really changed. You could see the passion, engagement, and trust drain from all those people who had been thrilled at the promise of a culture where collaboration and teamwork were at the core.

Great Teams Are Diverse Teams

Today's business climate is incredibly complex. We face disruption at every turn. The consumer is incredibly fickle or, at the very least, difficult to predict. No one person, no one style, no one skillset can effectively address the volatility of the marketplace.

That's why it is essential to build and maintain a high-performance team, a GREAT team, so you can effectively navigate these waters. We hear so much about diversity in teams these days, and I believe we need to look at diversity at all levels. We need to build and maintain teams that are:

- Culturally diverse
- Ethnically diverse
- Gender diverse
- Cross-functional
- Cross-divisional

The key to this diversity is not only in the hiring and retention, but also in the nature of the organizational culture. It is critical to have the right team, but just as critical that they are in an environment where they are encouraged to communicate openly and share perspectives. Remember the Culture Flywheel: the people, the organizational structure, and the processes must all be aligned to establish and maintain high performance. This applies 100% when it comes to ensuring you have access to the diverse perspectives within your teams.

Your diverse teams will look at challenges and opportunities through a myriad of lenses. They will not be myopic, but instead will see a multitude of problems that might otherwise go unnoticed or unaddressed.

Most of our decisions are driven by our unconscious, so to change the paradigm we need to consciously STOP, LOOK, and CHOOSE the best option. That likely involves increasing our awareness by consulting other people and sources. This was the case with the team on the digital supply chain. How would we possibly build the Fox Media Framework without pulling in a cross-divisional team?

Also having a diverse perspective will provide better input for a better solution. It's a simple formula: **Better Awareness → Better Choices → Better Results.**

Unconscious Bias

Earlier, we discussed how people develop fixed beliefs over time, and how those beliefs become our reality. Fixed beliefs generate filters through which we see the world. Eventually, they create an internal library of video recordings that unconsciously drive our thinking and our behaviors. This unconscious bias is a key topic in today's world. Events and experiences in our lives lead us to draw conclusions and reinforce stereotypes that may in fact be wrong. In order to counter this unconscious bias, we must take conscious steps that will directly improve our approach to diversifying our teams.

It starts with encouraging diversity of input around who we hire. Otherwise, we might be likely to hire mini versions of ourselves rather than others with complementary strengths, which may not be in the best interest of diversified viewpoints. We might also not pick the best person for the job because of our unconscious bias about who excels at what.

As we build our teams, we need to ensure we take steps to avoid letting our unconscious bias drive our decisions.

Last but Not Least, Embrace Your Teams!

After spending 11 years at Disney, I moved on to the role of CFO for Fox Filmed Entertainment. With the challenging culture at Disney, I was looking for a change, and I immediately knew on my first day at Fox that I had found it.

Jim Gianopulos, the co-chair of the studio, walked into my office, gave me a big hug, and said, "You are the CFO. You can attend any meeting – join any project here at the studio. You do not need to ask permission." This was a major shift for me. For the first time in a long time, Finance was being invited to the table.

Here I was on day one of my Fox tenure, and the chairman was empowering me, clearly indicating I was a valued member of his team.

Chapter 5

An Open Culture and the Value of Feedback

"The single biggest problem in communication is the illusion that it has taken place."
— George Bernard Shaw

"Communication, the human connection, is the key to personal and career success."
— Paul J. Meyer

"Feedback is the breakfast of champions."
— Ken Blanchard

Just like we took steps to have an open, trusting group on the task force when we established the digital supply chain vision, we wanted to set up Enterprise Operations as the poster child for cross-divisional teamwork. We wanted the studio to see Enterprise Operations as a service group that aspired to add value to every one of our divisions and to be selfless in the process.

In order to do that, as I mentioned earlier, the group needed to be open to a process of continual improvement. The team needed to be transparent so that the operating divisions could have complete visibility into how customers were being serviced, and needed to listen to others' perspectives about how they could improve.

To accomplish this, Enterprise Operations needed to be transparent and open within its own ranks. When we built the team, we pulled in people from the different studio divisions, including Technical Services, and had them initially continue in the roles they had been performing. However, that meant that each of these subgroups was continuing to service its prior division and was not necessarily focused on the best approach for the overall enterprise.

As we have discussed, we all have our fixed beliefs and fixed behaviors. Some of them are formed when we are very young and drive our attitudes and actions for much of our lives. But we also develop fixed beliefs and fixed behaviors from experiences in our current environments. So, when these subgroups came into Enterprise Operations, they were still carrying the inherent biases instilled during the time spent in their respective divisions. It was only natural.

There were strong convictions within Home Entertainment based on their experience serving large retailers, within Television Distribution based on their experience servicing broadcast and cable platforms all over the globe, and within Technical Services who participated in some ways with both of those groups. Even the leadership for each Enterprise Operations subgroup was reluctant to give up what they believed were the best practices they had used in the past.

To address this, we brought the Enterprise Operations subgroups together, starting with the leadership team, to share perspectives openly and discuss how to improve our overall service to the organization. This process didn't always take place organically. Our beliefs and attitudes can be strong and polarizing. We exchanged feedback with each other to communicate what was in the way of moving the division forward. We worked hard to create a *safe environment so that the team could share these perspectives openly and elegantly.*

However, there was a point in this process where we had a complete breakdown. The leadership team was at odds over how best to move forward, and we were stuck. Frustration was rampant, and I came to realize that the breakdown was all the way at the top – in the leadership team itself. If we wanted to move forward, we were going to have to make changes.

This was a pivotal moment for the group. I had personally been involved in establishing this leadership team for Enterprise Operations. Every one of its members had deep knowledge of supply chain and a great understanding of overall operations.

Even though everyone was saying all the right words around teamwork and collaboration, those themes were not playing out effectively across the group. Some of the leadership team was still locked into the ways of their respective division's old physical supply chain, and just couldn't seem to step beyond that frame of reference. As a result, some of the Fox divisions didn't feel that the group was hearing their concerns.

This was an emotional decision for me for multiple reasons. Here were leaders, some with a long tenure at the company, who had performed exceptionally well for years and for whom I had great respect, whom we had pulled away from existing roles and hand selected as leaders for Enterprise Operations – and now we had to undo it. I felt it was unfair to them because we were possibly derailing career paths. I was also concerned that this might provide ammunition to the operating divisions that already believed Enterprise Operations did not know what it was doing.

At the end of the day, I knew we had to make the changes. It was the only way I could see to shift Enterprise Operations back into a process of continual improvement and truly create significant ongoing value to the entire studio.

I knew it was risky. Under the prior leadership, we hadn't elevated Enterprise Operations sufficiently. The legacy Home Entertainment people were sitting with the Home Entertainment division all the time, the legacy TV Distribution people were sitting with TV Distribution, and the legacy Tech Services folks were still with their group. We were yet to create an open culture where the groups could come together and really transform the operation.

After making the changes, we transformed to a point where each of the Enterprise Operations groups was open to the idea that we needed a new approach – a more collaborative approach. We believed we now had the right people in place, but we realized we needed to go further. We needed to refer to the Culture Flywheel and address the next key component: the organizational structure.

The new Enterprise Operations leadership team didn't hesitate to restructure the group. They decided we could no longer afford to operate in subgroups that were structured solely along the lines of business we were servicing. It was too siloed. So, we restructured the group into three areas: Physical Media to service the legacy DVD retailers, Digital Media to service both Home Entertainment's and Television Distribution's digital platforms, and Research and Analytics to evaluate the processes of each of the other two groups. We utilized the research and analytics as a tool to drive continual improvement. With these changes, people on the team were no longer separated into groups that could just be loyal to their old masters.

And as to my fear that announcing the change in the leadership team would provide ammunition for the operating groups to question Enterprise Operations' competence? It was completely unfounded. The divisions lauded the change, saying it was a brilliant move. The groups knew the new leadership would create a collaborative culture and drive the changes that would most benefit the overall organization.

AN OPEN CULTURE AND THE VALUE OF FEEDBACK

Often, breakdowns can be catalysts for dramatic breakthroughs. Sometimes we cannot see the possible breakthrough while we are in the midst of breakdown, but I have seen it happen over and over again. Breakdown, breakthrough! It parallels the phrase "Out of chaos comes opportunity."

The restructuring ended up being a game changer. Now that we had shifted the people and organizational structure, we could effectively address the third and final component of the Culture Flywheel: the processes.

Even though I did not have experience in supply chains, I had formed beliefs about the best way forward, and while those drove my behavior, not all of them were on point. For example, I was convinced that we needed an overall digital supply chain across the enterprise, and that we would be best served to build and grow it as quickly as possible. We were at a point where we were finding a rhythm in improving our processes and having few exceptions in delivering our materials to our customers. And the culture was now very open, with team members feeling comfortable sharing ideas and building on them. One of the process ideas that generated a lot of traction was expanding Enterprise Operations to include the rights management function— and it seemed like a great opportunity, so I pushed the team to move quickly.

Rights management information addresses what rights the studio has for each film and television property and goes hand in hand in determining where studios will distribute materials. For decades, the Television Distribution group had overseen rights management. They had been the logical custodian because for all that time they had distributed products in sequence after Theatrical and Home Entertainment and had tracked all the activity of those divisions that came before them.

During that time, Television Distribution had always had visibility into film and television rights around the world, so it wasn't surprising that they felt they were the rightful owner of that information. But now the world was changing. With the onset of video on demand, digital sell through, and streaming, the release windows for our product were no longer sequential. Now that we had centralized the mastering and distribution of all materials, it made perfect sense to me that Enterprise Operations should oversee rights management as well.

As I mentioned before, the big difference between the shared services projects at Disney versus Fox was the mandate. Tom Staggs, Disney's CFO, had come into the room and said to the entire group that my authority over the decisions was final. He basically told everyone in the room, "This is the way it's going to be – Dean has the final word."

At Fox, you recall, I asked the chairman if I could lead the project. He said yes, and then I had to not only go figure out how to do it, but also determine how to get people behind it. He never formally stood in front of the room and said, "Dean's in charge of building the supply chain," or anything like that. He just said, "Sure. Go do it. I'll support you." It was essentially having the responsibility without having the official authority. In the absence of complete authority, I had to build influence and generate alignment.

To build that influence and alignment when we were first establishing Enterprise Operations, we spent many cycles educating the operating divisions on how the group would be formed and operate. We went through a lot of questioning and pushback, and I felt we had lost valuable time. So, when we were looking to roll out the rights management piece, I did not want months of delays.

Now remember, feedback can be an incredibly powerful tool. We all have blind spots. Many members of the Enterprise Operations team had blind spots based on beliefs they had formed over many, many years. They believed they were right in making their decisions, believing their way was the best for the organization, and it often required feedback for them to see beyond those beliefs. I had blind spots too and could have used some feedback myself.

AN OPEN CULTURE AND THE VALUE OF FEEDBACK

I was so convinced everything we were doing was the right way to go that I did not believe anyone—or anything—should slow us down. So, without adequately socializing this next step, I pulled the trigger and announced the jobs for the new rights management team. Even though I did not have a mandate, this one time I acted like I did. And I lived to regret it.

A senior executive in Television Distribution heard the news and was livid. This individual felt I had betrayed their trust, and they were right. This executive verbally attacked me, both personally and professionally, accusing me of many things that were not true. But it didn't matter at that point. After the confrontation, we literally did not speak to each other for months.

Eventually, we resumed communication, as it was important that we continue working together, but the damage was done. Our relationship was never the same. So, in this case, I had a blind spot, and I could have used some feedback to allow me to see things more clearly. Ultimately, I received the feedback, but it was hardly elegant.

When I joined the Disney studio in 1991, theatrical marketing was a whole new world for me. I realized quickly that the theatrical marketing team was a completely different breed of professional. For most of my career, I had been dealing almost exclusively with finance and accounting personnel. Now, I was interacting with marketing, creative, publicity, promotions, advertising, and research teams. I needed to speak a whole new language.

I realized immediately that I could not just come in and be the finance police. No one would want to talk to me. I needed to communicate in a whole new way. I needed to find ways to collaborate (not a word I used back then) so that we could work together to get the best value for our money without impeding the creative process.

For as long as they had been around, Theatrical Marketing executives were evaluated based on the magnitude of a film's box office opening.

In fact, the Marketing Department was in a business unit separate from the distribution group, and therefore did not have insight into a film's overall profitability. So, I needed to find a way to build their awareness of the overall value of a film, and the relative impact of marketing spend.

For the first time in my life, I learned to talk with creative and strategic marketers. I listened and learned how they viewed the key pillars of a marketing campaign so I would be sure not to undermine their creative efforts with any efficiency proposals. We worked together to find ways to drive costs out of our processes without taking away the impact of their marketing efforts. We negotiated volume deals and other special arrangements with vendors. We expanded third-party tie-ins to help offset our own marketing spend. We re-evaluated the impact of post-opening media spend. I was transparent in all of my communications so that it was clear I had no hidden agenda.

Working together, we became a team and worked as partners to create a process of continual improvement. The marketers and I saw the world through different lenses, so we created an environment of openness, where we would consider each other's points of view. We were willing to hear each other's perspective – knowing that our own perspectives were in fact not the only perspectives available. Through this approach, we achieved a high level of mutual trust and respect.

This transparent, collaborative approach differentiated me. I wasn't the typical finance guy. I learned to provide constructive feedback, and to be truly operational. This is the role where I found my business voice. I realized for the first time in business that who I am, not what I do, is what truly differentiates me – it is in fact what truly differentiates each of us. Learning to fulfill my responsibilities without impeding the creative process became an incredibly useful tool for me – and it became a key differentiator in my career.

AN OPEN CULTURE AND THE VALUE OF FEEDBACK

Seeing Through the Johari Window

To build relationships in Disney Marketing and with the Studio CFO, I needed to demonstrate that I was open and transparent, and to establish an open communication channel for giving and receiving feedback around any fixed beliefs and behaviors that might be counterproductive.

In order to establish and maintain an open culture, people must be open and authentic. A tool I use in coaching leaders into greater effectiveness, awareness, and authenticity is called the Johari Window. The name "Johari" is an amalgamation of the first names of the psychologists who created it, Joseph Luft and Harrington Ingham. Established in 1955, they created the Johari Window as a framework for understanding people's relationships to themselves and to others.

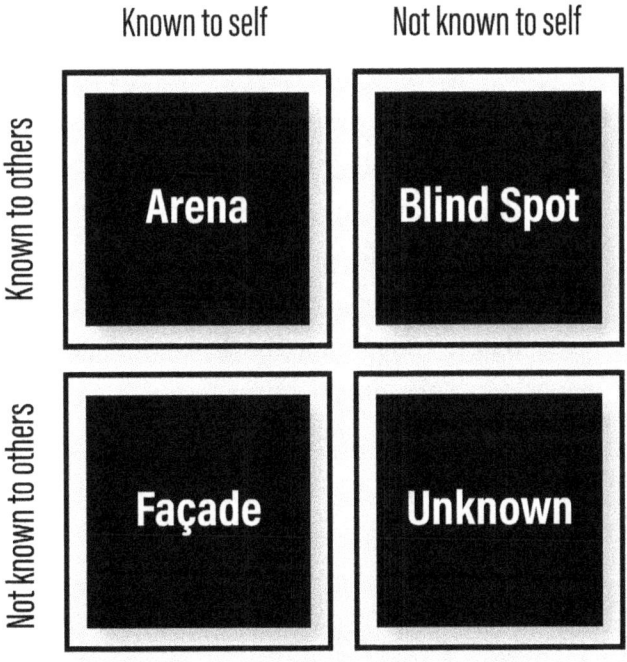

On the X-axis you have what is "Known to self" and "Not known to self." On the Y-axis is what is "Known to others" and "Not known to others."

The "Arena" is what I refer to as "my public self." That's the "self" I put out there for the world to see. I'm OK with that part of me. Other people see it, and there's no inconsistency with how I see it myself.

The box right below the Arena is called the "Façade." This is what I call the "private self." That's the part of me that I hide from the public. It's where the secrets and skeletons lie. It's what I consciously or unconsciously don't want to reveal to others.

Then there are my Blind Spots. These are the areas of myself that I *don't see*, but that others might know about me. An example of this that I learned through feedback is that when trying not to hurt someone's feelings, I can come off as cold. That isn't my conscious intention. Through feedback, I have realized that in my effort to not hurt someone's feelings, I can withhold my own feelings and empathy, which can lead to the perception that I am uncaring. As a result, when I am trying to spare someone's feelings and treat them with *more* dignity, I may actually end up doing just the opposite. This feedback gave me an opportunity to learn a good lesson about something I had been doing unconsciously for a number of years. It was a Blind Spot, but I have worked to overcome it. I can consciously choose to connect with someone and let them know that I care, because that is more important than my trying to spare their feelings. Ultimately, I can share what I have to say in a way that fosters dignity, mutual trust, and respect. The person receiving the feedback can then choose how they feel about it. It isn't my right to decide how someone else should feel.

Finally, the "Unknown" box, or the Mystery box, as I like to call it, is really just a big question mark. Nobody knows what is really there. What's interesting is that when you lay the Johari Window on top of Maslow's hierarchy of needs, you see what's really going on. When people such as Maslow are striving towards self-actualization, they're really unpacking the Façade and Blind Spot boxes to get a sense of what's inside themselves.

My experience leading major corporations and coaching executives is that as people get feedback, they can take some of that new insight and shift things from the Blind Spot box into their public self. This is possible because now they're aware of these things, and they can *see* them. And, as they're willing to share more of their private self from the Façade and be more open and transparent, they shift those items into their public self as well. Maybe it doesn't go completely into the public Arena, where it's in full view for everyone in the world to witness, but it certainly does broaden the span of people with whom they are willing to share those parts of themselves.

The combination of these two shifts seems to create a positive vacuum. I don't claim to fully understand the science behind it, but as you move things out of the Blind Spot and the Façade boxes into the public Arena box, you start to learn more and more about yourself. It's a process of ongoing self-discovery. I encourage people to be open to feedback and to be open with me as their coach. As we work together to shift things out of the Blind Spot and Façade boxes, we're going to learn new things about ourselves.

Feedback – The Least Expensive, Most Valuable Management Tool

Since Maslow's era, cognitive neuroscientists have found that we are conscious of only 5% of our cognitive activity — leaving the remaining 95%

of our feelings, activities, decisions, and behaviors to our unconscious minds.[9]

It may be difficult to compute just what percentage of the day we spend in full awareness of ourselves and our surroundings, but we *do* know that if average awareness rests at 5% of our activities, a small increase in that awareness could be a key element in high performance. Therefore, putting some attention on increasing awareness may be well worth our time.

As I have said, we all have blind spots. We can only correct them when we are aware of them. What faster way is there to become aware of our blind spots than for another person to point them out?

If we don't point out each other's blind spots, we are actually doing our colleagues a disservice. This disservice not only affects the individual, but it also disrupts the organization as a whole. Conversely, when we provide constructive input for others in a trusting environment, we promote a more open, collaborative culture. This, in turn, encourages everyone else to be better and to be a catalyst for improvement. Such a culture fills in *The Missing Piece*: high-performance leaders at all levels, which in turn leads to high-performance organizations.

Now, I understand that giving and receiving feedback may not always be a pleasant experience. After all, sometimes the input can be hard to hear. That's why it's important to emphasize that the feedback is not personal. It's not a value statement of who somebody is. It is just one person's perception of another at a given time and place. The feedback may not even be accurate. That other person's perception may be flawed due to their own filters, opinions, and belief system.

---

9   Marianne Szegedy-Maszak, "Mysteries of the mind." *US News World Rep*. 2005 Feb 28;138(7):52-4, 57-8, 60-1. http://webhome.auburn.edu/~mitrege/ENGL2210/USNWR-mind.html

However, if several people in the same organization or department have the same feedback for a particular individual, it would be helpful for that person to consider their role in creating such a common perception of themselves.

With a minimal increase in awareness, a person becomes capable of noticing opportunities and patterns that they didn't see before, and leveraging these new perceptions into insight, strategy, and effective plans. It is in these cases that breakdowns can be addressed early and develop into constructive and productive breakthroughs.

Developing Trust Through Open Communication and Feedback

The process of giving and receiving feedback increases levels of mutual trust and respect. Initially, many people fear rejection, failure, shame, and embarrassment when giving or receiving feedback. This makes sense because we filter the information that we receive with both our subconscious and conscious mind, and we're wired to only let in the things that are consistent with our own belief systems. When we are presented with something that is in conflict with our belief systems, our defense mechanisms kick into high gear. However, if we are at least 1% open to the fact that there's something new for us to learn in the feedback or in another's point of view, we might come to see things differently as a result. This is all part of the Discovery Model that we teach in our Accelerated Leadership Program.

Feedback, if delivered constructively and elegantly, will be viewed as something team members welcome. No longer will they fear rejection or humiliation. No longer will they be afraid to speak their minds or honestly share about each other's weak areas and blind spots. In fact, teams will do their best work when they don't hold back on giving honest and constructive criticism.

The next time you believe you might spare someone else's feelings by withholding valuable feedback, stop for a moment and ask yourself if you are actually doing that person a disservice. Look for new ways to provide feedback effectively in order that the recipient might see things more clearly. Then you can become a catalyst for building high-performance leaders in a high-performance organization.

Be At Least 1% Open

Every new ALP cohort that arrives for orientation on a Monday morning is sure to have its fair share of skeptics. And who can blame them? Most of us have listened to enough dry PowerPoint presentations and empty platitudes about "mission" and "purpose" that we don't need to hear another one.

So, it is certainly understandable for people to be reticent at the outset of an ALP training experience. In this context, the word *reticent* may be taken as a synonym for "closed off." That's why I always encourage new students in the art of leadership to be at least 1% open.

In one memorable installment of ALP, we had an amazing contributor. Let's call her Amanda. Amanda was full of creative and innovative solutions for many of our company challenges. However, she also implied to the group that she had more life experience than everyone else and, therefore, had less to gain from the program.

By conveying this message, Amanda was effectively communicating to others that they needed the program more than she did. In doing so, Amanda didn't realize that she was unintentionally isolating herself from the rest of the group and creating the perception that she was distant and arrogant.

A few months later, I led an exercise intended to promote feedback within the group. During the exercise, Amanda heard loud and clear from her peers that she had distanced herself from the rest of the team. Many of those giving her feedback thought she came across as cold and aloof. Others commented that they didn't feel as though she was part of the team.

Were Amanda's feelings hurt when she received this feedback? Absolutely! But this was not simply due to the nature of the feedback she received; she was actually *more hurt* because she felt *blindsided* by the feedback.

Amanda had worked with the other participants for months to solve multiple business issues. She felt that she had built good relationships within her cohort. As a result, she felt betrayed by the group when this "surprise" feedback came. She felt the other team members had been dishonest with her all those months. From her perspective, she felt somebody should have cared enough to give her that critical feedback before it was too late.

Amanda also felt ripped off. Here she was in a program established to accelerate the leadership skills of its participants, yet no one had shared this difficult yet constructive feedback with her. I recall her reaction vividly. "Why on earth would you wait five months to tell me? I could have been working on improving [this blind spot] all this time!"

According to an article entitled "The Importance Of A 'Feedback Culture' – And How You Can Build It In The Workplace" published by TruQu, one of the best ways to raise employee morale and develop a positive workplace environment is by establishing a "feedback culture." When employees experience psychological safety in the workplace and receive permission to express their thoughts about their organization, morale and engagement increase.

The article claims that roughly 50% of the American workforce feels disengaged, and only 16% feels actively connected and engaged with their organizations. The article then references an Engagement Institute analysis estimating that the annual economic cost to companies around the world for *disengaged or under-engaged* employees is a staggering $500 billion.[10]

Feedback is an incredibly valuable tool for increasing employee engagement and can drive significant economic value in virtually all organizations.

---

10 "The Importance of a 'Feedback Culture' – and How You Can Build It in the Workplace." TruQu, November 11, 2019. https://truqu.com/en/blogs/the-importance-of-a-feedback-culture-and-how-you-can-build-it-in-the-workplace/ .

AN OPEN CULTURE AND THE VALUE OF FEEDBACK

Leadership Close Encounter – All Leaders Leave a Wake

I often coach executives not to take everything personally. I know this is sometimes easier said than done.

I had often seen studio chairmen challenging executives in different ways, and often times the executives would leave the interaction feeling dejected, sometimes even personally attacked.

In one telephone interaction, a studio chairman jumped on my case about an oversight in one of the areas I led. I tried to explain to him the details and background, but each time I started to speak, he pushed back harder. I felt like the more I tried to defend myself, the further I was sinking into quicksand. Finally, I just let the chairman finish what he had to say.

For several days, I just couldn't let go of the conversation. Against my own best advice, I had taken the interaction personally, so I promised myself that I would look for a time when I could meet with the chairman to discuss the call.

After about two weeks, I found the opportunity as I sat across from him in his office. I told him I wanted to discuss the "bad call" we had, to which he responded, "What call?" I gave him some background to jog his memory, but to no avail. I told him clearly the call left a much greater impression on me than it did on him. It became clear that during our call, he said what he wanted to say and then moved on. I should have listened to my own advice and not taken it so personally. This chairman had moved on and was still a huge fan of mine. I was the only one continuing to carry the weight of the conversation.

All leaders leave a wake, sometimes good and sometimes bad, but the individual also plays a role in interpreting its impact.

People Really Do *WANT* to Hear Your Feedback

It's natural for people to want to avoid conflict. Most of the people I know are truly caring and compassionate team players. So why should we impose ourselves on others by providing difficult feedback, creating potential conflict, and causing ourselves discomfort? Why should we offer feedback if it could potentially hurt someone else's feelings? Why should we ever subject ourselves to the blowback of others who might possibly reject what it is we have to say? Why shouldn't we just avoid all that conflict, keep quiet, and keep ourselves safe?

The answer is…

Your Organization's Health Depends on It!

Organizations are only as good as their people, and feedback is one of the least expensive yet most effective management tools we have available to us as leaders. If certain behaviors or actions are getting in the way of peak performance and no one is providing feedback to address those issues, then the team is actually holding the organization back. The longer the behaviors and actions go unchecked, the greater the drama will be when the "Be nice" dam ultimately breaks, just like it did in the story about Amanda. *So, how do we get over this uncomfortable hurdle?*

In short, we need to change our perspective. Most individuals who withhold feedback claim they are doing so to spare the other person's feelings; however, in reality, the withholders are typically just protecting themselves from potential conflict, and in doing so, are actually *harming* the other person. The truth is that feedback can be delivered in a constructive way, one in which it can actually build mutual trust and respect and truly benefit the other person.

AN OPEN CULTURE AND THE VALUE OF FEEDBACK

Tips for Giving More Effective Feedback

There's an old parable about a farmer who in his zeal to profit from the harvest pulled on his crops every morning in order to speed up their growth. The plants withered, and the harvest never came. Openness is like that crop. It simply doesn't work to tell members of a workforce to *be open* because it's a company priority. As a leader, you must help shape the culture.

Instead of attempting to mandate openness, set time aside for managers to exchange ideas and give constructive feedback to their teams. Then make sure to create systems and structures for managers and leaders to communicate feedback horizontally with each other. Openness forms the foundation to get people collaborating.

Remember this: the pace of the leader, the pace of the team. If you want to create a culture of openness and honest communication, the best thing you can do as a leader is to share information about yourself and begin to ask for feedback. Find someone who cares about you enough to give you an honest assessment and clear feedback on a regular basis. Your example will help to create an open environment that is safe for everyone. That's when feedback will start to become natural. People won't feel threatened because they'll know it's being used as an effective, constructive management tool. Your vulnerability as the leader will protect the environment.

Here are some quick guidelines for giving effective feedback. It should be real, timely, honest, empathetic, and aimed at mutual growth. When it is, the recipient is likely going to be far more receptive to it and far less resentful, especially where this feedback might otherwise be hard to hear. When feedback is provided on a real-time and ongoing basis, it can actually keep communication and perspectives open and help cultivate positive outcomes proactively. This helps to extinguish negative feelings harbored among team members. When we withhold our feedback, it is a disservice that not only hinders participants from improving in their blind spots, but also leads to distrust, resentment, and division within the overall team or organization.

We Are Better Together than We Are Alone

The value of feedback for both those giving and receiving is that it fosters a culture of empowerment. Sharing information about yourself can be empowering for others and inspire more feedback. Even though you may not want to give somebody else difficult feedback, remember that by doing so, you'll build trust at a deeper and more meaningful level. You can create a safe environment and have a constructive dialogue about the situation, allowing you to fully address the issues. When handled properly, you can dramatically reduce the likelihood the recipient will be defensive about receiving the constructive feedback that you're offering.

Organizations thrive when team members give honest feedback and share essential information about themselves and their areas with one another. Openness can be empowering and can inspire teams to become their best. Having your team support and encourage you is an amazing feeling, and you can experience this feeling of empowerment whether you're a leader, manager, or participant. Knowing that you have team members who support you on that level is incredibly powerful. You'll also have increased confidence because you'll know that you have invested in your team and helped them grow. When this happens, they'll be willing to do whatever it takes to get the job done. They'll believe in you and trust you more.

Communication Leads to Collaboration and Innovation

When you have an open culture, people will be more collaborative. When they're more collaborative, they will be more creative because they are letting their ideas flow. When you generate more creativity, as a company you are going to be more innovative. That's the path to high performance.

In the end, listening to the feedback was transformational for Amanda. Literally two weeks after that exercise, her boss came to me and said, "I don't know what you did with her, but she is an entirely different person. She is amazing, and everyone wants to work with her." Once she recovered from the noise around it, the feedback Amanda received was truly a gift.

Chapter 6

Collaboration and Empowerment

"Coming together is the beginning. Staying together is progress. And working together is success."
— Henry Ford

"The truth is that teamwork is at the heart of great achievement."
— John C. Maxwell

"If you want to go fast, go alone. If you want to go far, go together."
— African Proverb

There were three or four people with me at the center of the Digital Media Framework who were rock solid, and great team players – a core group responsible for the direction and energy of the overall project. All of them encountered resistance and experienced frustration in their efforts to keep things moving. We became a tremendous support group for each other. Any of us could call the core group together in a room at any time to collaborate, get focused, and get back on track.

I know my communication breakdown with the Television Distribution executive wasn't something that was going to be turned around in a week or two, but we needed to keep the project moving forward. I went to the head of Enterprise Operations and said:

"Look, just continue talking about Enterprise Operations and the Fox Media Framework with TV Distribution. Don't mention my name as it will only add fuel to the fire. That group has great respect for you, and you are truly pushing what is best for the company. Collaborate with them and let them know you understand and appreciate their concerns, and that you will work constructively with their group to address any issues. If you tie yourself to me, you're going to get all kinds of unnecessary flak."

Some people have told me that this approach demonstrated a high level of emotional intelligence. Honestly, to me it was just common sense. Why would I want to insert myself as an obstacle when what we were trying to achieve was so important?

We strategized on who should communicate with whom in the business units. It wasn't always easy. At times it was downright messy. We forged ahead as best we could, building trust and alignment day in and day out.

We relied on shared vision and management. We aligned the team. We continued making personnel changes in areas where people would not come into alignment. We established open and honest feedback loops. These are all leadership tools — and we used them. Not only did we use them; we also taught these tools to our middle managers so that they could more effectively lead their teams and inspire collaborative teamwork.

Over time, Enterprise Operations established a very open and trusting culture, and the group inspired significant collaboration. As you recall, the overall goal of our cross-functional team was to design and develop a single digital supply chain that would replace each distribution group's separate physical supply chain. The group had now come together to meet all of our vested interests, serving and supporting the entire studio organization to be the best it could be.

We had taken people and groups that had been operating very independently and trained them to work as high-performance teams. These teams now trusted each other enough to build on each other's existing ideas and continually collaborate on new ones.

The truth is that in developing a high-performance, collaborative team in Enterprise Operations, we were a bit lucky. For years we had been bringing cohorts of people through the Accelerated Leadership Program, including many people working in Theatrical, Home Entertainment, TV Distribution, and Tech Services. As a result, when we formed Enterprise Operations, the group included several ALP graduates. These graduates knew the value of an open, collaborative culture, and their presence accelerated the group's transformation. These leaders spread the vision and transformed the culture of the entire operation, particularly as we expanded into new areas.

We were in a position to take on even more and add greater value. We established procedures to smoothly effectuate the continuing transition from physical to digital. Physical media wasn't going away anytime soon. After all, the industry still controlled tens of billions of dollars in physical media revenues, but the relative weight of each of the businesses was shifting, and the group's resources and innovation needed to shift with it.

With a more collaborative culture, the respective leaders of the physical and digital groups worked together to game plan the transition of resources as the digital media world continued its growth. These key group leaders grasped the true meaning of high-performance leadership. They became vested in each other's success and worked together for the benefit of the overall supply chain organization, and in the process elevated their leadership to new heights. They exemplified the leadership we worked so hard to develop at Fox. They walked the talk.

Despite my faux pas in handling the shift of the rights management responsibilities, together we raised the Enterprise Operations performance to a whole new level. We began identifying endless possibilities for improving the Fox Media Framework's contribution to the overall organization, far beyond just the studio.

Building the Fox Media Framework was a massive feat, the success of which relied on a shared vision, empowered leadership, collaborative teamwork, and creative innovation. We had multiple departments involved, including Theatrical Distribution, Home Entertainment, Television Distribution, Technical Services, and all of their international extensions.

Had we not developed the centralized digital library in a collaborative way with the appropriate "connective tissue" to the larger operating groups, we never would have been able to make the project a success. We were better together than alone, but it wasn't easy. It took commitment, diplomacy, and the special talents and knowledge of everyone involved. And even with all that, it was still messy at times, but the team delivered.

So how did we build this kind of collaboration into the process? It all started by training and developing our people.

My decision to leave public accounting in 1988 was a pivotal moment in my career. I had anticipated being a lifelong partner with Ernst and had not really developed any contingency plans. I had no Plan B. The idea of leaving public accounting was scary. Up to that point, it was all I knew. I had no tangible idea how I would contribute in private industry. Sure, in public accounting I interacted with individuals in private industry all the time, but that was as an outsider looking in, and I knew I was only getting glimpses of the true day-to-day operations of my clients.

A colleague introduced me to a recruiter who placed candidates exclusively at The Walt Disney Company. The prospect of working at such a large, public organization was daunting. Disney had started its upward trajectory under Michael Eisner and Frank Wells. The company was thriving – optimizing the impact of its intellectual property through all of its divisions. I would be such a small minnow in a massive ocean where I could easily drown. Fear of failure was not a normal feeling for me, but my career trajectory through public accounting had always been in my comfort zone. Now, the fear of failure was very real. Nevertheless, I readied my resume and prepared for my interviews.

An Unexpected Opportunity

Luckily (I believe), prior to going all the way down the Disney path, I received an offer from one of my public accounting clients—a recreational and industrial product manufacturer)—where I was hired as the Pools Group Controller. The Pools division had a very small and nimble management team, and we all wore a number of hats. I learned to work effectively in a team that collaborated in nearly all areas. I learned things from cash flow to sales and marketing to how to build a pool better-cheaper-faster to product liability for alcohol-induced diving board accidents.

I was empowered to take the reins, seize opportunities, and solve problems, and I learned to contribute in significant ways. I remember when the oil market collapsed in the late 1980s and homeowners in Texas lost virtually all of the equity in their homes, to the point where they could no longer qualify for home improvement loans. The lack of access to credit was killing our business in the region.

I was tasked to meet with every Dallas bank I could access to develop creative financing arrangements for our customers. With the trust of the rest of my management team, I had full authority to put a program in place. We developed creative loan packages with multiple banks in the region, which led once again to our business thriving in Texas. These experiences, with the collaboration and trust of the team, empowered me and taught me to be agile and proactively add value.

The Courage to Be Yourself

Ultimately, the pool industry was not the be-all, end-all for me. A former Ernst colleague of mine had gone into the head-hunting business and he also had his foot in the door at The Walt Disney Company. This time, I was excited at the prospect of working at the large entertainment conglomerate. I now knew how to create results in an organization, both individually and through a team.

However, rather than trusting my instincts and being myself, knowing I had essentially not interviewed for a job in roughly ten years, I allowed the recruiter to instruct me on my interview style and approach. I tried to follow the recruiter's prescription step-by-step, but it wasn't natural for me, and I completely blew the interview. Somehow, though, the hiring VP saw enough promise to invite me back for a second round. At the second interview, I made a commitment to myself to do the interview as authentically as possible and to be vulnerable.

To me, vulnerability is the courage to be myself irrespective of the outcome. I knew that disclosing what had caused me to blow the first interview could put me at risk of losing the opportunity, but I was willing to put it all on the table. When I walked in the door, I immediately confessed to the hiring VP how I had mishandled the first interview, and the honesty of that moment solidified my relationship with him – more evidence that authenticity is what sets us apart and creates connection, an essential element in collaboration.

Collaborate for Survival

Collaboration can quite literally save your organization. Take for instance the lesson in this story: *There once were two groups of ants. The first group decided it was best for each of the ants to scatter and fend for themselves. But the second group decided to work together for the benefit of the overall team.*

The first group seemed to start out well. Each ant went out and searched for just enough food to meet their own individual needs. Each individual was feeling strong and independent. But then it happened. The individuals began to realize that there was great competition for the food. No one cared about the other. Each ant was focused on its own well-being. Soon, egos began to inflate, and chaos ensued.

The second group, however, did not immediately scatter. Each team member was encouraged to push aside its pride and admit its weaknesses along with its strengths. With pride aside, a few clear leaders rose to the top of the group. Those strong in searching were sent out to find food. Once they returned with their discovery, each ant took its designated place in line and worked together to pass the food from the source back to the hill. A few ants became discontented, feeling their talents were not being used effectively, so the leaders stepped in and encouraged them. The leader ants trained them in more efficient ways to transport the food, and the leaders gave them the necessary tools and equipment to get their jobs done easily.

This was very helpful for most of the discontented ants. Instead of being negative, they began to feel empowered, encouraged, and motivated to continue their work and reach the group's vision. The few ants that stayed negative left the group of their own accord and joined the first "group" of scattered ants. They soon regretted their decision. At the end of the day, the first group was frustrated, separated, and angry. Some ants were left severely injured from poor working conditions while other ants were wounded by their infighting and countless battles against each other.

Getting in Their Own Way

Their goal to fend for themselves was thwarted by... well... themselves. They left broken, bruised, defeated, and worst of all, still angry and hungry. The second group, on the other hand, returned to their anthill at the end of the day feeling good about their work. They were proud of what they had accomplished as a team, and they shared the fruits of their labor as they reflected on a job well done.

Ample provisions were gathered, and each team member was able to take satisfaction in contributing to the benefit of the whole. You see, thanks to the efforts of their leaders, each ant in group two understood its role. These ants felt empowered and recognized and knew that they were part of a larger purpose. They began to see how uniquely they were each created with different skills, strengths, and talents. They were confident in their roles, knowing that they were positioned in the perfect spot on the team to contribute and shine. Realizing they were stronger together than they ever could be individually revolutionized the way they viewed their work. Instead of fending for themselves, their goal was to gather enough food for the group to sustain all lives.

Their team-centered approach made achieving that goal attainable. Their realization of a necessary dependence on each other created a culture of success through teamwork, collaboration, and empowerment. Best of all, the collaboration model the ants operated in was the natural way to function.[11]

I recently came across that short story and wanted to share it with you here because I think it makes an important point.

The Hidden Cost of NOT Training Your Team

As I mentioned in the introduction to this book, I remember a cartoon drawing from a business publication featuring two executives arguing about training their employees. The stick figure CFO said to the stick figure CEO, "But what if we train them and they leave?" to which the CEO replied, "What if we don't train them and they stay?"

The decision to train and invest in your people doesn't have to be this complicated. One of the greatest benefits of training your people is

---

11 Adapted from https://wesgay.com/parable-of-the-ants/

employee engagement and retention. Yes, your people will become more marketable, and some of them may end up leaving you. But I've found that, by and large, the opposite is actually true.

When you train your team, they will feel more connected to the company and will know they're valued because you took the initiative to invest in them. If they learn collaboration and become a collaborative leader, they will be able to take their contributions to a whole new level and will actually become *more valuable* to the company.

Lessons from the Accelerated Leadership Program

In the ALP Program, we spend hours upon hours discussing the benefits of collaborative leadership and connected teams. In one particular program, the participants brought their focus to the area of brand management, and suggested we were missing opportunities. If you think about a movie over its entire lifetime—and not just the movie, but marketing, distribution, multiple channels, possible video games, and other spin-offs—you have a lot to think about.

Yet, we weren't doing enough of that across the company. We weren't establishing a narrative arc over the life of each property. Instead, each business unit had been making separate, independent outreaches to its customer – a customer that likely engaged with several Fox business units over the course of a product's life. As these customers were hearing independently from multiple Fox units, they were likely receiving mixed messages rather than a consistent narrative established for each specific brand or franchise. This magnitude of this issue was growing as the sequential nature of release windows over the course of a product's life was diminishing.

Several members of the Fox leadership team had identified this challenge and knew that we needed a more collaborative approach. We needed a solution that would set up each property as more than just a theatrical movie. We needed to think about the properties in terms of their overall universe and mythology, and build a solid foundation for linking all elements to that brand. So, one of the ALP project teams took on the challenge.

The ALP team knew that to build a solid foundation for a piece of intellectual property that the entire company could get behind, it was critical to bring in representatives from each of the Fox units. The input from all the groups was essential.

Theatrical Marketing had always been charged with opening each movie to the highest possible box office. While box office can be a predictor of the overall performance of a film, it is not the sole driver of ultimate profit for the underlying property. Film marketing teams understand this, but the idea of bringing others into their process posed a threat – the threat that they might lose control of the initial marketing message. Their theory was: *You only get one first impression!*

Forming a Brand Management Group

Giving consideration to those concerns, the ALP team recommended we form a comprehensive Brand Management group to build on the early-stage Franchise Management team I mentioned earlier, and assemble a cross-divisional task force at the beginning of each new brand or franchise launch. These task forces included representatives from each Fox group that would likely be involved at some point in each of the underlying intellectual properties. In most cases the task force was assembled before we even green-lighted the movie so we could talk about the various goals and needs of each business unit. We would ask things like:

- *What is our vision for this movie?*
- *Why does this movie matter?*
- *How do we want to market it?*
- *What is the overall narrative arc over the life of the intellectual property?*
- *To what media formats does the property lend itself (movie, tv, videogame, book, etc.)?*
- *Who are all the critical participants and departments we need involved?*
- *To whom are we marketing it?*
- *Who is our audience?*

By thinking through these questions with the right folks, we were able to have a clear vision of what we needed to accomplish, like: *How we can take our audience on a journey over the life of this property. What elements we need to launch the film effectively. What we can use to tease the Home Entertainment launch and expand the film's overall audience. Whether this movie can lend itself to a video game. Whether we can leverage an effective consumer products campaign.*

Back then, Fox didn't have the depth of Disney's brand and franchise infrastructure. Disney made huge investments in brand management as they acquired Pixar, Lucasfilm, Marvel, and others. However, the Fox brand management efforts did make a difference in how we approached our products because they elevated our strategy beyond selling movies – they brought consumers into a bigger universe, promising them a more special journey or experience.

More than just selling movie tickets during a film launch, we were elevating our game in creating a new level of engagement with our consumers across the entire lifecycle of the film. Much of this gained traction through a project and presentation that the ALP Program initiated – a project that focused on collaboration across different parts of the company.

This Fox example shows how collaboration can drive effective change in a company and enhance the company's ability to compete effectively in the market with a piece of intellectual property.

Collaboration Across US Joint Special Forces

General Stanley McChrystal is an outstanding example of a leader who successfully managed change and developed his mid-level officers into collaborative, high-performance leaders during his tenure as commander of the Joint Special Operations Task Force in Iraq. Central to his effort was creating an environment favorable to trust and open communication.

I once attended an event where General McChrystal was a speaker. His description of events during the Iraq War has stayed with me all this time. He shared that upon taking command of the Joint Special Operations Task Force, he became aware that he had a unique challenge on his hands: US Special Operations forces were better equipped and trained than Al Qaeda insurgents, and winning nearly every battle they fought… yet the US was still on a trajectory to lose the war.

The Al Qaeda network was decentralized and nimble. Situations evolved very quickly. Intelligence also emerged quickly and would need to be acted upon quickly – a pace that the Task Force struggled to get ahead of. As a result, the US Forces initiated missions on average only once a month.

A key obstacle to beating the nimble, adaptive, and fast-moving Al Qaeda network lay in the Task Force's culture. While each individual unit embodied trust, collaboration, and open communication within its own group, there was insufficient communication and trust among different units and agencies. They were siloed from each other, and therefore unable to respond nimbly, adaptively, and quickly to the enemy.

Modeling Desired Change

Recognizing the operational need for an organization that could outrun, outthink, and outmaneuver the enemy, General McChrystal reimagined his Operational and Intelligence Morning Briefing from a daily ritual for select senior commanders and unit leaders, to a daily two-hour intelligence-sharing video conference open to every member of the Task Force, at every rank.

The purpose of the meeting was not for McChrystal to be able to micromanage his team, but to be able to facilitate information sharing. It was also about his *thinking process* regarding how to approach challenges at hand – instead of attempting to solve problems himself. If someone on the call asked what the general would do in a particular situation, his response would go something like this: "I cannot say for certain what decisions I would make. I am not on the front lines, and I don't have all the information. However, based on what you have shared, here is how I would think about it…" This approach empowered everyone on the team to share, take the initiative, and collaborate with teams outside their units.

Collaboration over Territorialism

This daily video conference famously grew to thousands of individuals in attendance. Once the entire team grasped how the general thought through issues and challenges, they could align themselves with that approach, and be empowered to make timely decisions on the front lines.

After shifting the culture, the Special Forces raised the frequency of US-initiated missions to an average of one or more per day. The result of the group's openness and transparency turned the tide in the war.

Organizational change begins with people. Like General McChrystal's example, change requires leaders to model openness, transparency, and trust in ways that elicit increased trust and collaboration from members of their team.

Hearing General McChrystal's story certainly made me curious about film marketing teams' reticence to collaborate with other divisions based on concerns over losing control of the marketing message. The Special Forces were sharing complete intelligence across thousands of individuals with our national security at stake. If they can collaborate, I see no reason why divisions within an organization cannot do the same.

Leadership Close Encounter – Disempowering Your Team

During my tenure as a Group Controller, a senior executive was very hands-on and was often overly critical of members of the Pools Group management team. It seemed important that he regularly argue that he had a "better idea." He worked incredibly long hours and questioned the commitment of others who didn't follow his lead.

At various points in time, this executive and I discussed the successful management team at the Walt Disney Company. We talked about the power of the Disney brands and the endless opportunities to leverage their incredible intellectual property. He even went so far as to tell me, "Now that is one company I would love to work for!"

So, when I told this executive I was leaving for Disney, I expected he would be excited that I had such an opportunity. Instead, he proceeded to tell me I was making the biggest mistake of my life and went on and on that I would never be successful there. He implied that had it not been for him, I wouldn't even have been successful in my Group Controller role.

Rather than building the strength of his team, this executive came from the command-and-control world and held himself out as the only catalyst for anyone's success. Ironically, not too long thereafter, he was asked to tender his resignation.

Collaboration Is the Art of Leadership

Great collaboration is the art of working with others to help shape and form what you are trying to accomplish for the good of the larger organization. When your team is open to collaboration, you can lead in a way that makes the others better. Team members will work toward a common vision because collaboration is about working together and pushing each other to be their best. When this happens, everybody wins.

I personally do not agree with the Peter Principle, which states that people rise to their level of incompetence. Rather, I believe they rise to the level just beyond that for which they have been trained. In my experience, most people are trained and developed as individual performers, but they are not trained to lead teams. That's where the breakdown usually takes place. Too many people rise through the ranks as individual performers, and not much more beyond that. That's where people run into trouble, and that is where the need for collaboration comes in. True leadership is leading and empowering your team to collaborate and work effectively together. That is the art of leadership. Collaboration is about empowerment. It's when you're looking to develop people and have them work collectively to their fullest potential.

Middle Managers

To truly establish a collaborative environment, you must engage your middle management. You want to communicate to them that they have a voice to be heard and that they matter. These people will become your champions for positive change. That's why we frequently focus our Accelerated Leadership Program on middle management. Sure, the leadership attributes we teach apply to senior leadership as well; however, middle managers can drive collaboration from within the organization as opposed to trying to drive it from the top down. And middle managers are hungry to learn more. Most are just starting to oversee teams and have not been trained in how to be effective in their new roles. These new managers don't have locked-in beliefs and behaviors that they want to defend. They are typically more than 1% open to new ideas and approaches on how to manage effectively. When you train them, they tend to be more open to collaboration. They become sponges for high-performance strategies. If you teach them the art of leading and collaborating, they can then pass that behavior on to their peers and their departments from inside the ranks of the organization.

The BE-DO-HAVE Model

Collaboration thrives with a BE-DO-HAVE model, meaning it is less about specific activities, and more about authentic behavior.

Most of our lives we are programmed to approach our lives as:

DO (work hard) → **HAVE** ($) → **BE** (happy) From the Work Ethic

OR

HAVE (BMW) → **DO** (what you want) → **BE** (happy) From Advertising

Although these two strategies are engrained in our goal setting and daily activities, if we stop and think about it, they don't really work. Does wealth guarantee happiness? Are workaholics happy? Does owning your dream car ensure a fulfilled life? These are based on a paradigm of chasing a desired future. On the other hand,

BE → DO → HAVE

can be very effective. This approach is not about activities or possessions. In this approach, what you do and what you have are the byproducts of who you are. This paradigm is based on where you "come from," and I don't mean geographically. It is based on how you *show up*. If you come from a place of authenticity, and create human connection, you can choose to do and have the things in your life that support who you are. You can choose to change attitudes, beliefs, behaviors, or actions to achieve desired experiences.

If you want team members to trust each other, work together, and collaborate effectively, the team members need to be authentic. The more you lead from your authentic self, the more the people around you are going to trust you, and what you communicate is going to resonate more with them. Team members will be more likely to actively engage in projects and work collaboratively with you in order to reach your overall goals.

The greatest benefit to following the BE-DO-HAVE model is that it develops stronger bonds among team members. It harnesses collaboration and draws out as much of the team's creativity and intelligence as possible. In addition, middle managers who forge strong personal bonds with their peers across an organization will retain those bonds and habits of collaboration as they rise through the leadership ranks. This leads them to forge long-term cultural shifts across the organization in the quest for openness and collaboration. When you foster collaboration with your middle management champions, they adopt that behavior and spread it to everyone else in a positive way.

Leadership and Empowerment Foster High-Performance Teams

I can't say it enough. Leadership is about fostering an environment of collaboration. The leader creates an environment where people can collaborate; where people can be coached to work effectively in teams. When the leader empowers the team, the framework for high performance is in place. The team will work together like a highly tuned machine. Your team members will be invested and engaged in the success of your organization's mission.

Members of collaborative teams also feel increased accountability to their teammates. They take an increased sense of personal responsibility for each other's performance, which translates into an organization's performance. If you generate a level of engagement where people feel they are part of what is happening, they will be more willing to work together. They will be inspired because they see the vision, and they will feel empowered to pursue it. No longer will they feel they are just doing a job for the salary. Instead, they will view their work as meaningful.

They will know that what they have to say matters because healthy communication and collaboration go hand in hand.

When people know they will be heard, they will automatically be more open – more open in dialogue, giving and receiving feedback, and sharing ideas. This will naturally lead to more effective teamwork and greater creativity and innovation. Best of all, they will feel more empowered, and empowerment means they will be loyal to you and your company.

Chapter 7

Creativity and Innovation

"There is no innovation and creativity without failure."
— Brené Brown

"Imagination is a force that can actually manifest a reality. Don't put limitations on yourself."
— James Cameron

"Imagination is everything. It is the preview of life's coming attractions... Imagination is more important than knowledge."
— Albert Einstein

Once we firmly established an open, trusting environment that fostered collaboration, Enterprise Operations really shifted into overdrive.

With the right leadership at the top of the group and a supportive environment in which management truly wanted to hear the team's ideas, the team fully aligned around its vision. People could feel the desire for collaboration and began expressing their ideas for areas of improvement. We finally arrived at a place where we had a process of continual improvement; where we were constantly throwing out ideas about what else Enterprise Operations could do that would bring value not only to the overall studio, but to the entire Fox organization.

We truly were committed to a process of continual improvement. It wasn't just lip service. We constantly challenged the status quo. And we constantly asked ourselves:

- Where can we drive greater efficiency?
- How can we improve our processes?
- Where can we increase automation to reduce human error?
- What other Fox companies outside of the studio can leverage our services?

The creative ideas constantly flowed. The group felt safe in raising new ideas and each member was open to other people's input on how to improve them. There were so many ideas, in fact, that we had to prioritize where we could drive the most impactful innovation. Let me give you a flavor for some of the key innovative ideas that we implemented.

In the physical supply chain world, studio customers had paid for the media tapes that the studios provided, which included replication costs for each of the units produced. In the early days of digital media, most of the platforms had proprietary requirements for the format and specifications of each digital submaster file produced specifically for them.

In order to reduce the number of unique files we generated (in line with our vision), the team developed a standardized file format and offered it FREE to any customer. After all, any customer that would accept the standardized file format would be one less customer requiring physical tapes or a unique file format. For every customer that would accept the standard file format, we could further simplify our operation.

With the introduction of the standard file format, the adoption rate for digital media files skyrocketed. The standardized file actually became a *standard for the industry. Sure, Fox paid for the master file, but we had virtually no replication costs, so the overall financial impact to Fox for providing the file was significantly positive.*

There were many nuances in the international operating arena, including commercials of variable length on the broadcast and cable platforms. Creating the international files to accommodate the varied structures required significant manual labor. The group worked together to develop systematized processes that would auto-generate the foreign episode files, including all of the necessary foreign language tracks and/or subtitles.

We also conceived, designed, and built a proprietary delivery network over the internet that allowed us to easily move our files anywhere they needed to go. This aspect of the Fox Media Framework provided tremendous agility and substantial cost savings. While such a network is more commonplace today, one did not exist in the industry at the time.

So, when 20th Century Fox TV made the shift to broadcasting series episodes on the same day and date with the USA in all major international territories, Enterprise Operations made it possible. In the physical media world, there just wasn't a sufficient runway to complete an episode, prepare formats for all of the worldwide outlets, and then deliver the materials in time for a global airdate. The calendar was just too tight. There had always been a frantic rush to dub or subtitle episodes at the last minute, and now the Fox Media Framework gave us enough time to execute.

When the creativity and innovation were firing on all cylinders, it felt like magic. We proactively and reactively began developing and implementing capabilities that in the early days weren't even in our consciousness. We stumbled across other opportunities we hadn't ever considered.

For example, in 2009, the world had not yet fully transitioned to digital cinema in the theaters. As such, we were still shipping physical film reels to several countries around the world. On one of our key tentpole films, the post-production team was late in finalizing some of the international versions.

In order to manage piracy, Fox had been striking some of the high-risk-country film prints in the USA under tight supervision and shipping them to the local territories for distribution to specific theaters. At that time, one of these key territories had a very cumbersome customs process, and even with Fox personnel accompanying the shipment, there was no way the prints would be delivered to the theaters by the film's release date. We had worked with the film post-production team when designing the Fox Media Framework, including both the duplication and delivery protocols to ensure we could accommodate theatrical distribution needs once the digital cinema rollout was complete. But this was a scenario we hadn't anticipated.

We needed to digitally deliver the necessary international theatrical print master, from which the territory film reels would be generated, to an in-territory film duplication facility, where the Fox team would be waiting to oversee the process and ensure our materials wouldn't be pirated. This approach had never been taken before. Film print masters had never been transported digitally. We put all hands on deck, determined the necessary protocol for making a seamless digital delivery, and avoided a huge catastrophe in the process. The lessons from this exercise not only elevated the credibility of Enterprise Operations and the Fox Media Framework, but also had a significant impact on profitability, which we will cover in the next chapter.

Success begets success. Even though we built the Fox Media Framework and the related digital vault specifically for the film studio, it was quickly recognized as a key strategic asset that could benefit the entire organization.

When Fox made an acquisition, Enterprise Operations onboarded the new company's film and television library into the digital vault and supply chain. We built a backup facility in Las Vegas that could supply our customers worldwide if LA operations were interrupted for any reason, such as an earthquake. *As word traveled and Fox grew through acquisitions, our Fox Media Framework became the go-to digital supply chain for the enterprise.*

In 2019, Fox sold its studio to Disney. It's my understanding that key elements of the Fox Media Framework were some of the only Fox systems and technology that Disney adopted because they had nothing like it – no one else in the industry had anything like it at the time.

By all accounts, the 2009 blockbuster movie *Avatar* was a huge success. During its run in theaters, it broke several box office records and became the highest grossing film up to that point in time. It was nominated for nine Academy Awards, including Best Picture and Best Director for James Cameron.

Although the movie was not released until 2009, Cameron's first treatment for *Avatar*, outlining the world of Pandora and its myriad creatures, was written as early as 1994. Film buffs will note that this was before the 1997 release of Cameron's record-breaking *Titanic*. Once Jack and Rose's story had been cemented in the hearts and minds of theater-goers worldwide, there was talk of releasing *Avatar* in 1999. Even so, it would take another ten years for the movie to make it into cinemas. This begs the question: *why?*

The main reason for *Avatar's* lengthy development is that Cameron's concept was far ahead of the technology of the late 1990s, making it unrealistic at that time to bring the story—as it had been conceptualized—to the big screen. After wrapping *Titanic*, Cameron had begun looking into the capabilities of computer graphics (CG) technology, including technology to transform real actors into on-screen avatars. However, he quickly conceded that the technology available at that time wasn't up to the task, and he put the project on hold while he waited on technology to catch up to his vision.

In the interim, Cameron turned his attention to documentaries, including *Ghosts of the Abyss* and *Aliens of the Deep*, in which he utilized and further developed digital 3-D filming techniques. Cameron refined these techniques for their eventual use on *Avatar*.

While waiting for the filmmaking world to catch up to his breakthrough ideas, Cameron also benefitted from the conversion of movie theater projection technology from analog to digital, which included photo-realistic 3-D capabilities.[12]

The Essence of Creativity and Innovation

It's often said that necessity is the mother of innovation. But even beyond that, I believe innovation starts with imagination. A great example today is Elon Musk and his innovations with Tesla, SpaceX, and the Boring Company. True innovators imagine new ways are possible. When they see problems that force them to innovate, they embrace the challenge and never give up on their vision.

This was the case with Cameron. He knew the technology was advancing rapidly and, through trial and error, he was able to pioneer what is now called motion capture animation. Cameron also innovated new ways to capture sound, body movements, and lighting for massive stage areas like those used for Pandora's jungle scenes.

This new motion capture technology broke the barriers of stop-motion animation and replaced it as the new standard for Hollywood. With his many successes, it's undeniable that James Cameron is a modern master of creativity. He has consistently been way ahead of his time.

---

12 Craig Elvy, "Why the First Avatar Took so Long to Make," ScreenRant, August 29, 2019, https://screenrant.com/avatar-movie-development-long-reason/.

Culture Drives Creativity and Innovation

As with everything we've covered so far, an organization's culture is often the primary driver of its results – including its creativity and innovation. As I discussed in "Chapter 1: The Importance of People," an organization that aligns its people and implements processes to support the functioning of a new organizational culture becomes nimble and capable of responding quickly to changes in the marketplace and regulatory environment. In addition to responding, such nimble and responsive cultures are even capable of initiating and *driving* new changes in the marketplace and regulatory environment themselves.

This is what happened with Cameron and 20th Century Fox, a studio that had earned the reputation of being a great partner to film producers and directors. Its culture was absent the corporate control mentality of so many rival studios, which allowed Cameron's creative process to thrive.

Another example was Fox's partnership with Lucasfilm, which was extraordinary. The level of detail and coordination necessary for these two entities to collaborate on the first two *Star Wars* trilogies was phenomenal. Maintaining the mythology and providing a seamless marketing campaign took Herculean efforts on both sides. But again, Fox's intense focus, creative collaboration, and authentic leadership culture paved the way for a thriving partnership that led the industry to new heights.

Creative Ideas Can Come from Anywhere

The bottom line is innovation is the expression of a company's culture. Innovation cannot be transplanted into an organization. It cannot be bought. It cannot be mandated through speeches and work sprints. It must truly grow from within the interior of an organization.

Said another way, innovation emanates from people who trust each other and communicate openly. This includes your introverts and extroverts. Some of the best ideas are in the hearts and minds of your introverts, and you definitely want to bring those forward. When you create a safe environment for all people to collaborate, you invite the presence of everyone's creativity into their midst. The creative spirit that emerges in conversations, meetings, lunches, and team projects becomes an organizational tendency of innovation that drives success. Unfortunately, when a trusting and aligned culture isn't in place, the reverse effect is true. A negative or unhealthy culture stifles creativity.

Negativity Kills Creativity

That's why I say the number one obstacle to creativity is negativity. For this reason, it's essential to continue the ritual of constructive feedback exchange to discharge any negativity that gathers like dust throughout the office. Once openness and collaboration are established, the path in the workplace is clear for the emergence of creativity, and creativity in turn generates a harvest of its own.

For instance, when we're collaborating and listening to others, we tend to be less protective of our own ideas and less territorial about our department's resources. After all, if we've been collaborating robustly over time, we have seen for ourselves that another person's participation can improve our own ideas. For example, I might say, "I'd like to do X." My colleague from another department might say, "Great idea! Have you thought of achieving X through Y and Z?"

Developing creative ideas through collaboration and innovation generates a special kind of momentum. Imagine a large wind turbine that takes a few moments to rev up. When it finally does get going, it's almost unstoppable. It's the same with creativity and innovation. The healthy velocity that's generated is a magnificent, vibrating pitch that attenuates the energy in the room, and people at this stage are much less guarded than they were when they began their journey together. They speak up regularly and discuss all facets of the idea or subject at hand.

Creativity Empowers the People in the Trenches

As we establish ALP training cohorts, we often focus our attention toward the "troops on the ground." These people are your middle managers and their teams. They live on the front lines of your company's day-to-day operations. They interact with your customers and clients the most and, therefore, they have the potential to notice changes, new opportunities, and anomalies before anyone else.

It may be fair to say that middle managers and their respective teams are typically *more* limited in their views than senior leadership, which rightfully tends to focus on larger trends, patterns, and priorities. Most middle managers are focused on a particular lane and their own view of the terrain they are facing. However, when you bring *all* middle managers together to exchange new ideas and experiences, you are likely to end up with an incredibly valuable 360-degree view of your company's ground-level operations.

Then, collectively, you can challenge these managers by inviting them to articulate that 360-degree view and present their ideas directly to senior leaders.

"Some of the Freshest Thinking in Years"

The presentation of new ideas from within the ranks of your organization is the window through which many *new products of innovation* are likely to emerge. The feedback loops you encounter from these presentations can inform what you need to "KEEP-DELETE-CREATE NEW" for your company's future direction.

The whole point of fostering an open, collaborative culture, ripe with constructive feedback and effective communication, is to drive greater creativity. Yet it's not just creativity for creativity's sake. As we've seen with the examples from *Avatar* and *Star Wars* at Fox, creativity leads to breakthroughs and innovations, and breakthroughs and innovations lead to profits. That's why I would set my focus on engendering communication and collaboration among your organization's diverse individuals, all with different roles and responsibilities within your company. Creativity will likely emerge.

Hallett Leadership's Accelerated Leadership Program does, in fact, follow this model. As I have mentioned earlier, at the end of each ALP cohort, small cross-divisional, cross-functional teams present to senior leadership. The challenge for each team is to develop an innovative solution, process, product, or other output intended to enhance the company in some way.

When a version of the ALP program was in place at the Fox studios, a studio chairman enthusiastically stated that members of the ALP teams presented some of the freshest thinking he and the senior leadership team had seen *in years*. This was because of our creative commingling of new ideas.

Normally, ideas are generated in a single division, limited by the lens, priorities, and biases of that division, but ALP presentations are always conceived and presented by people from different divisions and disciplines. Therefore, ALP recommendations arise from multiple perspectives and focus on the best interests of the company as a whole.

According to Diego Rodriguez, a partner at IDEO and the leader of its Palo Alto, California, office, most innovations today draw on many contributions.

"Consider the examples of InnoCentive, of Mozilla, of Wikipedia," Rodriguez said. "All are contexts that bring in lots of contributors. And the fundamental structure of such networked organizations is not centralized and top-down. People don't do what they do because someone told them to do it. Contributing to an interdependent network is its own reward." Rodriguez argued forcefully that, even in today's highly networked world, organizations fail to take full advantage of internet technologies to tap into the creativity of many smart people working on the same problem.[13]

Leadership Close Encounter – Who Asked You?

In 1994, shortly after my promotion to VP of Finance for Disney's Theatrical Marketing unit, we were working on the campaign for the Broadway launch of Beauty and the Beast. In a marketing meeting with 20 executives, I was the sole Finance representative.

Launching a stage play in one theater was a completely new challenge for a division that typically launched films in thousands of movie houses around the country. During this meeting, I suggested an approach to the campaign that was immediately praised in the room as a great idea. But the senior marketing executive in the meeting quickly interjected and turned to me to say, "Yes, that is a great idea, but we are not looking for those kinds of ideas from Finance."

This was not the only time this person disparaged suggestions from my division. This individual operated from the hierarchy of a command-and-control style, not in an authentic or open way, and lost out on many great ideas because of it.

---

13 Teresa M. Amabile and Mukti Khaire, "Creativity and the Role of the Leader." Harvard Business Review, August 1, 2014. https://hbr.org/2008/10/creativity-and-the-role-of-the-leader.

Excellence vs. Perfection

As noted previously, negativity kills creativity. When coming from Perfection, we leave no room for mistakes. As soon as something goes wrong, things can no longer be perfect, and anger and frustration will often immediately follow.

As an alternative to demanding Perfection—*or always striving to be right*—coming from Excellence means striving to be *the best one can be,* and for the larger organization, *to be the best it can be* moment to moment.

Our daughter Makenzie said her marriage vows in 2018 on a bluff overlooking the ocean. It was an elaborate affair, with many details planned for the day and evening, and I know she wanted it all to be perfect. At the beginning of the day, I conveyed to her that with all the variables at play, something would most likely go wrong over the course of the day and ceremony. I explained that if she focused on that one detail gone awry, she would take herself out of the moment and miss the truly special, once-in-a-lifetime experience that was before her.

As we began walking down the aisle, Makenzie was extremely nervous and emotional. I urged her to just immerse herself in the experience – reminding her that all of these people were there because they loved her.

Maybe it was Murphy's Law, but as I was handing her off to our future son-in-law, one of us somehow tugged on her veil and pulled it off her head. Her maid of honor tried feverishly to put it back in place, but with the ocean breeze, it just wasn't going to happen. Makenzie, realizing this, removed the veil completely, and at that moment shifted into coming from Excellence. She instantly realized she could only do her best from that moment forward, and immediately embraced that attitude. She quickly relaxed, owned the joy of the moment, and truly immersed herself in the experience… and had the time of her life. She truly shined.

Being *the best you can be* starts with one thing: being honest with yourself. This is especially true in cases where we have been wrong or failed at something. Instead of treating failure as the "to-be-avoided-at-all-costs-terminal-resting-place," an Excellence mindset treats failure as the first step in a learning sequence whereby new skills and insights are developed that can advance the person or company along the path of becoming the best they can be.

The learning sequence can be divided into three parts:

1. Accepting failure
2. Rapid-response learning
3. Integrating lessons and moving forward

We coach this three-part sequence in more detail through ALP, but the take-away is Excellence leads to breakthroughs and new possibilities.

The key value of such breakthroughs is self-evident, as people, processes, and the organization as a whole stand to benefit from learning and improving. But one of the positive side effects of coming from Excellence is relieving the worker from the stress of demanding Perfection.

Excellence keeps companies vital and dynamic. Companies that foster an Excellence orientation among their people empower each individual to take risks and speak up when they have an idea or see that something could be improved.

Senior leaders who follow an Excellence orientation themselves are willing to lay their egos aside and listen to new ideas coming from anyone in the organization, regardless of their rank – unlike my experience with the Disney Marketing senior executive.

This is what Ray Dalio famously calls leading with an "Idea Meritocracy." It's a system that brings together smart, independent thinkers and has them engage in a healthy debate, where they productively disagree in order to drive the best possible collective thinking, which then enables senior leadership to decide on the best way forward.

Leadership, Creativity, and Innovation with an Idea Meritocracy

True leadership moves creativity and innovation to the forefront of an organization. Creativity empowers people to come up with new ideas on their own and empowers people to pursue them. I can't reiterate this enough: true creativity begins with your people. An aligned workforce is well positioned for moonshot thinking, innovation, and creativity of every kind.

Your only limit is the shared imagination and thought of your entire organization. If you were told that each individual in your company has potentially infinite reserves of innovative thought and creativity, what could this mean for your organization as a whole? It is easy to forget that in a fast-paced and at times stressful workplace, our company's greatest ideas are buried deep inside the hearts and minds of our people – including the introverts! Who knows, you may even be sitting on your own *Avatar* breakthrough for your industry.

The habit of innovation is simply the habit of eliciting your people's ideas on a regular basis. This is precisely what your management training plan should set out to accomplish. If setting time aside to get your people talking to each other and developing openness and trust seems too costly and inconvenient, just imagine how costly and inconvenient it will be when new companies suddenly disrupt your company and industry. Fostering innovation from among the ranks of your people—particularly your middle management layer—may be the optimal way to negotiate a volatile and disruptive marketplace.

Chapter 8

Profitability

> *"You have to talk about the culture before you can talk about business."*
> — Peter Lai

> *"Success and profitability are outcomes of focusing on customers and employees, not objectives."*
> — Jack Ma

> *"Happy employees lead to happy customers, which leads to more profits."*
> — Vaughn Aust

The Fox Media Framework had a tremendous impact on the Fox studio profitability. It all started with a need to provide a solution to deliver digital files to media platforms around the world to service our new video-on-demand deals. We knew that delivering files rather than physical media tapes would generate savings, but in the beginning, we had not anticipated the extent of the impact.

- We generated initial savings by eliminating the duplication and delivery of physical files. Ultimately, that change alone generated tens of millions of dollars in annual savings.

- *We shifted to a standardized file, nearly eliminating all customization for proprietary platform standards and specifications. That change also generated tens of millions of dollars in annual savings.*

- *In the previous chapter, I mentioned the solution Enterprise Operations deployed to deliver theatrical film prints in time for international theatrical releases. For key releases, Fox saved millions in customs and import duties. As a result, total savings over entire film slates again saved tens of millions of dollars.*

- *As noted in Chapter 7, the Fox Media Framework developed by Enterprise Operations enabled 20th Century Fox TV to move to a global day-and-date episode model. I cannot begin to estimate the impact of that service, but I know our deals with international broadcasters were much more valuable under the global day-and-date model.*

- *We also mentioned in the previous chapter that Enterprise Operations became the de facto service provider for onboarding acquired content libraries, avoiding significant costs that would have been incurred using outside service providers.*

As you can see, creativity and innovation can drive new business models, and those ideas can translate into significant profitability for an enterprise. It all starts with training and development – The Missing Piece *in most organizations. If you want to establish a high-performance organization, you must train and develop your team at all levels, where all members of the team can shift the overall organization into high performance. When you do, you will establish an open, collaborative culture where creativity and innovation thrive.*

Initiating the Process

Peter Chernin, former chairman of Fox, understands the value of collaboration. I had been with Fox only a few months when the company was deciding whether to offer Disney the opportunity to co-invest in the movie *Ice Age* and allow them to take over distribution of the film. Having spent 11 years with Disney and having been an integral part of the Disney-Pixar relationship prior to Disney buying Pixar, I knew first-hand the impact such a move would have on the Fox team.

We all clearly knew the potential value of a successful animated film, so the question was purely a creative one: *Did* Ice Age *rise creatively to the level of a blockbuster-animated film?*

I was a little surprised when Peter asked my opinion on the matter. I had only joined Fox a few months prior. I also wondered, since this was a creative decision, why Peter was asking *me* – I was the CFO. Sure, I had worked for Disney, so I could see things from their perspective, and I had seen this film, but Peter asking Finance to be part of the creative decision was counter to my experience at Disney.

I weighed in on Peter's question. I vividly remember my statement to him: "We would be crazy to give up half of this film and let Disney take over distribution. *Ice Age* is a great animated movie!" I know Peter solicited many different points of view, not just mine, but then that is the value of collaboration. Peter wanted a number of perspectives so he could have the best information possible to make his decision. And in the end, *Ice Age* went on to be the most valuable film franchise in Fox's history!

Peter's openness and willingness to collaborate led to greater creative and innovative input, and ultimately to greater profitability for the company. When organizations create environments of authentic leadership with clear alignment and foster a culture of creativity, collaboration, and innovation, profitability is a natural result.

Delivering Long-Term Profitability

Profitability is where it all comes together. In fact, without it, most companies will not survive for long. It is what most investors are looking for, as the value of an organization is often determined by a multiple of its earnings.

In today's world, the vast majority of people are looking for instant gratification. When it comes to profit, they are no different. Whether they are investors and stakeholders in public companies, or private equity and venture capital looking for a quick return, the pressure is on management to deliver profits without much delay. These factors place tremendous pressure on management and lead many senior leaders to emphasize short-term performance. When we focus on the short term, we are prone to making decisions that may be detrimental to the long-term success and viability of the organization.

To deliver long-term profitability, leaders must focus on delivering sustained value over time, and reinvent their organizations so the value they deliver to their customers doesn't diminish. To reinvent their organizations, they must disrupt themselves. After all, if companies don't disrupt themselves, others will do it for them.

Disruption Is Not a New Thing

There is so much talk about disruption now that it is easy to believe it is a fairly new thing, but it is not. History tells us that even without the pandemic, unrest, and recession, survival is a difficult task. Scholar Mark J. Perry has shown that 440 of 1955's FORTUNE 500 companies (supposedly the strongest and most powerful of their time) have PERISHED![14]

There are countless companies that have been unwilling to change their paradigm – unwilling to reinvent themselves. These companies have believed their products and services were immune to disruption. They have fallen prey to what is considered the Innovator's Dilemma, where businesses must choose between fulfilling their customers' currently prevailing needs and pursuing new technologies and business models to fulfill customers' future needs.

Most organizations find it difficult to let go of the current goose that is laying the golden eggs and lining their pocketbooks. They convince themselves that they can continue to differentiate themselves in their markets and remain relevant without evolving their offerings. They have their own set of fixed beliefs and fixed behaviors that they are ultimately unwilling to challenge. They have an overwhelming need to be right.

This attitude reminds me of an old limerick:

Here lies the body of Julian Grey,
Who died defending his right-of-way.
He was right, dead right,
As he droned along,
But he's just as dead as if he were wrong.

---

14 Mark J. Perry, "Fortune 500 Firms 1955 v. 2017: Only 60 Remain, Thanks to the Creative Destruction That Fuels Economic Prosperity." AEI.org. American Enterprise Institute, October 20, 2017. https://www.aei.org/carpe-diem/fortune-500-firms-1955-v-2017-only-12-remain-thanks-to-the-creative-destruction-that-fuels-economic-prosperity/.

Remembering Past Victims

There is a laundry list of companies that have fallen prey to resting on laurels and not innovating to remain relevant. Here are just a few examples:

Polaroid was founded in 1937 and was a leader in innovation. In 1972, the company introduced a new camera that produced a high-quality picture that you could watch appear before your eyes. As we approached the turn of the century, Polaroid believed firmly that people would continue to want printed photos, so the company opted not to participate in digital photography. Polaroid filed for bankruptcy in 2001.

The Xerox brand copying machine was so popular that Xerox became the generic name for all copy machines, and even a verb describing the act of copying. Then, in 1973, the Xerox company invented what is considered to be the first PC. However, the company believed a conversion to digital would be too expensive and was convinced that the Xerox company's future was all about copy machines. In 2001, Xerox was on the verge of bankruptcy.

Blockbuster was the dominant video-rental company. In 2000, Netflix proposed a partnership with Blockbuster that would allow Netflix to have a store presence in exchange for providing Blockbuster's online servicing. Blockbuster did not consider Netflix a threat, failed to innovate, and filed for bankruptcy in 2010.

Kodak was a household name for decades. The company actually invented the first digital camera in 1975 but chose not to move forward with it. Kodak feared disrupting its highly profitable physical film revenue stream. The company filed for bankruptcy in 2012.

Blackberry provided smartphones and offered the best encryption features, making the phones a hit with businesses as they entered the

21st century. When the industry began focusing more on user experience and larger screens, Blackberry believed that their advantage was intact. In 2017, Blackberry exited the smartphone hardware business.

Disruption Is Accelerating

We hear about disruption all the time. With the advent of new technologies, companies are facing disruption at breakneck speed. It doesn't even require technology companies to disrupt these days because technology change is so rampant and pervasive that tech-enabled companies are now doing the disrupting. Essentially, any company that can utilize a technology to create a direct connection with customers can disrupt an incumbent supplier. In most cases they can aggregate modularized suppliers at scale for the benefit of their consumers.

- Uber is not a technology company. It is a transportation company that utilized technology to massively disrupt the taxi and rental car industries.
- Airbnb utilized technology to aggregate vacant properties and scale worldwide.
- Google utilized technology to aggregate content providers.
- Amazon utilized technology to aggregate suppliers and distributors.

Self-Disruption = Innovation

In the face of all this disruption, it is essential to evolve and drive high performance throughout your organization and your people. Companies that don't evolve, that don't disrupt themselves, are likely to be disrupted by others, and in today's world may quickly perish. It is best to stay ahead of the competition and proactively disrupt your own organization on your terms.

In his bestselling book, *The Innovator's Dilemma,* Harvard Business Professor Clayton Christensen outlined the formation of innovation and technology.

Christensen, who first identified the importance of disruption in business, writes:

> *Generally disruptive innovations were technologically straightforward, consisting of off-the-shelf components put together in a product architecture that was often simpler than prior approaches. They offered less of what customers in established markets wanted and so could rarely be initially employed there. They offered a different package of attributes valued only in emerging markets remote from, and unimportant to, the mainstream.*[15]

Christensen's message is clear. The future belongs to the innovators. And you can bring innovation to your organization through increased collaboration and creativity, soliciting new ideas, rearranging product architectures, and trying new and unique combinations of products and services.

In the old world, pre-Information Age, it was the big that ate the small. But now, in today's world of rapidly increasing technology and innovation, it's the fast that eat the slow. You must disrupt yourself before someone else does.

Profitability Is the Result of Culture

Studies show that culture drives affinity to your brand. Based on an organizational alignment survey of 410 companies across eight industries, LSA Global found that *highly aligned companies…*

- *grow revenue 58% faster,*

---

[15] Clayton Christensen, *The Innovator's Dilemma* (New York, NY: Harper Business, 2011), 16.

PROFITABILITY

- *are 72% more profitable,*
- *satisfy customers at a ratio of 3.2:1, and*
- *engage employees at a ratio of 16.8:1*
- *... compared to their less aligned peers.*[16]

When leaders have a clear vision for their organizations and create alignment around it, opportunities abound. The collective group will identify areas for improvement, innovation, and greater efficiencies. On the revenue side, this will give rise to more creative direction and strategy. On the expense side, it will lead to greater streamlining, effectiveness, and teamwork. There is nothing sacred when the collective group is willing to look across the enterprise.

Always seek to create more engagement and empowerment. Think in terms of employee loyalty and retention rather than having to endure the cost of replacement. When you do, your people will be more invested in your vision and you'll profit as a result.

---

16 "How Organizational Alignment Creates Growth." LSA Global, April 21, 2021. https://lsaglobal.com/blog/organizational-alignment-creates-growth/.

Leadership Close Encounter – A Bad Plot Twist

Back in the late 1990's, Disney had developed and produced the film Sixth Sense, starring Bruce Willis and Haley Joel Osment as a young boy. The movie had a spectacular plot twist near the end, and the script read very well. Internally, the studio had high hopes for this live-action thriller.

While decisions were being made as to the financing and ownership of Sixth Sense, Universal Pictures released another movie starring Bruce Willis and a young boy: Mercury Rising. For all intents and purposes, Mercury Rising tanked at the box office. The movies were vastly different in concept and plot; however, fixed beliefs and fixed behaviors kicked in as the casting similarity was troubling to senior leaders.

Despite many studio executives being highly excited at the film's prospects, Disney—apparently in a show of little confidence in the film—sold the production rights to Spyglass Entertainment while retaining only the distribution rights and 12.5% of the film's box office receipts – representing only a minimal portion of the film's success.

The film Sixth Sense performed spectacularly, earning $673 million at the worldwide box office, filling the coffers at Spyglass Entertainment and propelling that company into a Hollywood player.

Kodak, the Phoenix Rising

I mentioned Kodak earlier in this chapter. Since the adoption of digital cameras in the early 2000s, the company has been lifted up as the laughingstock example of companies that don't innovate. They were literally too focused on what was established to recognize the new opportunities right under their nose. That now-obvious oversight led to Kodak's demise.

Like it says in the title of Marshall Goldsmith's book, *What got you here won't get you there*.

Kodak may finally be learning that lesson. After filing for bankruptcy in 2012, they retooled, innovated, and got back to experimenting in new areas. In the last several years, they have tried their hand at everything from home printers to digital currency.

Then in 2020, amidst the COVID-19 pandemic, it surprised almost everyone when then President Trump announced a $765-million loan to Kodak so that the company could manufacture pharmaceuticals to fight the virus.[17] While we don't know the future of Kodak's story, the lesson here can't go unnoticed. Constant innovation and disruption are the only way to sustain long-term success and profitability.

Better Awareness → Better Choices → Better Results

I believe it is the job of leaders to create organizational alignment and profitable growth. While most businesses strive for profitable growth, aligning all the critical factors to achieve consistent and highly profitable growth is not easy – but organizational alignment is worth it.

Having aligned teams simplifies the development and execution of strategy because information is shared more freely. Increased Awareness leads to Better Choices, which lead to Better Results.

Just remember, to truly increase your awareness, you have to give up your old belief system. This isn't likely to occur naturally. It requires investing in your people and letting them have a voice. This approach is a change for most companies, and most companies fear change. Yet, change is absolutely necessary to reinvent and disrupt yourself and your organization, and essential for staying on top of your game.

---

17 Cheddar Now. "How Kodak Is Reinventing Itself." YouTube video, 00:02:16. August 7, 2020. https://www.youtube.com/watch?reload=9&v=Xgolc4gcqMM

Transforming Your Company from the Inside Out

All too often, companies are looking to external resources for innovation. The truth is that in most cases, organizations already have the innovative resources they need – their people. Through your people, you can transform your company from the inside out. That's why we started this journey in Chapter 1 discussing the importance of people. As I said then, the #1 lesson I have learned in all my years is "It's the People!" Profits may be the end goal, but it always starts with the people.

You can transform your organization and your results by leading authentically, creating alignment, building the best teams, fostering open communication, and encouraging collaboration, creativity, and innovation. You will be nurturing your organization so that your people derive true meaning and satisfaction in their work, and you'll have clear alignment to power through obstacles and challenges. This focused vision will give you the driving force necessary to lead the competition.

The Impact at 20th Century Fox

When I came to Fox in 2001, we had great talent, but we had no employee development budget. This was understandably so, as austerity was high right after 9/11. We had a lot of really smart people, but we weren't investing adequate resources in leadership development.

So, we initiated leadership training and continued to build upon that training year after year. That's why I say it wasn't an accident that we proceeded to have eight consecutive record years, and nine out of ten. Cultural transformation is great; cultural transformation *with profit* is even better!

Conclusion

"Great things in business are never done by one person. They're done by a team of people."
— Steve Jobs

"What is powerful is when what you say is just the tip of the iceberg of what you know."
— Jim Rohn

"The only impossible journey is the one you never begin."
— Tony Robbins

At Fox, we purposely developed and trained our people so that they learned to collaborate as a team. Our chairmen participated and set the tone from the top. This had a monumental impact throughout the entire organization. The result was that we were able to take the company to new heights.

It all started with our people. People are the most valuable asset in every business. That's why it is so important you start with your people as the priority; it is always truly about the people. The people are your foundation.

Your people are not only the foundation for your cultural and creative success, but also of course your profitability. Having a great culture is wonderful. Having a great culture in an organization that is highly profitable is far better.

That's why I say...

You Must Be Intentional About Growing High-Performance Leaders

When you develop leaders at every level in your organization, you are able to determine your own corporate destiny. The future of your company lies in your leadership development program – or lack thereof.

High-performance leadership in every vertical, team, and department is what separates great organizations from merely good ones.

Some companies take the sink-or-swim attitude, while others just figure people will learn from osmosis. But both of those approaches can be recipes for disaster.

Intentional leadership development is the key differentiator in high-performance, highly profitable organizations.

Take Hold of Your Company's Future Today

That's the benefit of accelerated leadership, and Hallett Leadership's ALP program. Some companies claim they don't have time to develop and train their people. They claim resources are too scarce, or that they just need to run their businesses. Others are just plain fearful that if they train their people, they will leave for better opportunities.

That type of reasoning brings me back to the story I shared earlier about the CEO and the CFO: "The only thing worse than training your people and having them leave, is not training them and having them stay."

CONCLUSION

The truth is that developing your people and building a high-performance culture will allow creativity and innovation to thrive. People and teams will be more effective and efficient, which will free up time and solve problems.

In ALP, we teach leaders at every level in your organization how to "STOP, LOOK, CHOOSE."

STOP, LOOK, CHOOSE

The "Stop, Look, Choose" model is a framework for teaching potential leaders how to think about their appropriate response in any given situation.

Through real-life simulations in ALP, we teach managers how to:

1. **STOP** – Pause to consider the values, vision, and overall goals of the organization, department, or project.
2. **LOOK** – Turn to others for input for new ideas, innovation, and collaboration.
3. **CHOOSE** – Weigh the input from others in order to make the best decisions possible with the information they have.

By the time the program is over, these leaders understand the importance of authenticity, alignment, and feedback through honest communication. They understand what it means to truly show up.

They become equipped with the tools and training necessary to effectively lead at a high level in any area of the organization.

And best of all, their new approach will be integrated into their day-to-day leadership, and they will set the pace for those under their care.

Leaders Multiply Leaders

The benefits of ALP are felt immediately and are quite infectious. As soon as ALP graduates are put into new leadership roles, their subordinates, peers, and teams will catch on as these leaders model their new leadership behaviors.

High-performance leadership will start to spread organically among those who have not necessarily been exposed to the training firsthand.

In essence, the ALP leadership development program creates a farm team for not only *growing* new leaders, but also for *multiplying* leaders throughout your organization.

STOP, LOOK, CHOOSE works so well because it overrides the negative habits that so often have become automatic in stagnant institutions. And it overcomes the status quo that is so driven by the fixed beliefs and fixed behaviors we have built up over the course of our lives.

It is about being at least 1% open. It is about being authentic in the moment. It implies that to STOP and LOOK at the options available to us, we must listen to the perspectives of others. That dynamic fosters collaboration, teamwork, and greater levels of profitability.

Training Your People Is *The Missing Piece* to High Performance

Imagine your people coming to work each day, thrilled to be there, driven with a sense of purpose around a common vision.

Imagine different divisions of your company suddenly collaborating and communicating proactively with each other because they know that is the best way to get results for the overall organization.

Imagine your team taking creativity and innovation to new heights to problem-solve and proactively go after new opportunities.

CONCLUSION

Imagine your organization and its performance attracting some of the best talent in the industry.

This can be your reality.

Training and developing your people's leadership skills is what I highlighted in the introduction as "*The Missing Piece*" in most organizations. It is the component most often lacking.

That's why I want you and your team to learn what I have learned. While I spent decades mastering this approach, you can have access to all these benefits in a fraction of the time. No more skating by with mediocrity. No more wasting time with trial and error. You can put your company on the path to high performance and greater profitability right now.

This Is Only the Beginning

As we near the end of our time together, I want to say thank you.

Thank you for joining me on this journey where we've reflected on the qualities and benefits of high performance.

Thank you for allowing me to speak into your life and the life of your organization.

And thank you for being at least 1% open to the positive impact that you can achieve by applying these lessons.

The world needs more leaders. I am glad you and your organization are now on your way to accelerated leadership and filling in *The Missing Piece*.

This may be the end of the book, but it is only the beginning of your journey to high performance. The truth is your journey to high performance never really ends. Leadership development and continuous improvement are lifelong journeys.

Earlier, we talked about the Discovery Model and its impact. I can instruct someone on how to ride a bike, but there's nothing like the actual experience to integrate the learning. I put my heart and soul into this book to give you insights on how to approach high-performance leadership development, and the resulting impact; however, the lessons presented here will only take you so far. If you are serious about taking your organization's leadership to new heights, the Accelerated Leadership Program is the best vehicle I have witnessed. The program includes all of the leadership activities, facilitation, and hands-on coaching to get you there.

Our goal is to work with you and your team to take your organization to the highest levels of leadership and performance. This book is just the tip of the iceberg – a taste of how ALP can transform your business from the inside out.

Showing Up Authentically

I would love to work with your organization. I would love the opportunity to get to know you and go much deeper with your team, and so I've included this no obligation free offer. Simply go to my website at hallettleadership.com/register and sign up for the free bonus video series "Showing Up Authentically."

When you do, we will automatically process your information and send the link for your free three-part video training to the email address you provide. I'll also tell you how you can get more information for launching ALP in your company right away.

My goal is to help you reach these new levels of leadership and high performance. Don't just assume your company's people will learn leadership through osmosis. Don't be a culture where it is just sink or swim. Growth is a conscious choice, not a chance. Take action today – you'll be glad you did.

Afterword

Over the years, I have seen and participated in a multitude of leadership courses and workshops. While they all provide some value, the benefits of most programs just don't seem to last. The programs themselves tend to be too conceptual, and far too short. As a result, the inspiration from these programs dissipates far too quickly.

With his Accelerated Leadership Program (ALP), Dean uses a foundational approach to high-performance leadership: establishing organizational role models that can collaboratively develop a vision, and then influence and align people around that vision. This, he teaches, is how you create a team that consistently gets it right. It relies heavily on investing in and developing people *at all levels* of your organization to build a strong culture that can succeed and grow. Dean refers to this practice of developing leaders *at all levels* as *The Missing Piece* in most organizations today.

I met Dean in 2020, just weeks into the COVID-19 lockdown – when the collective global heartbeat slowed. In what felt like an instant, the world as we knew it seemingly stopped, pivoted, then flipped entirely. Amid tragic loss of life, many of us began re-examining the lives we lived, both personally and professionally. There was an unmistakable, shared understanding that the path forward was uncertain, and forging ahead was at once daunting and necessary. It was a time when I was already preparing for a career transition into my first CEO-level role. Suddenly, though, I was navigating it amid unexpected and extraordinary new dynamics.

To actively prepare for the professional challenge, I began a search for an executive coach. Dean was recommended to me by his former colleague and one of my close and highly respected professional and personal mentors, John Janclaes. Dean and I were an immediate match, and I soon began regular one-on-one coaching sessions.

Although much around me seemingly stopped, I began working with Dean to move forward and grow. Among the lessons I quickly learned from his frameworks and processes was the powerful idea of connecting personal growth and emotional intelligence with career and business development. I came to understand from Dean the superpower of authenticity – using sensitivity, vulnerability, and humility to turn up the effectiveness of my leadership.

My work with Dean generated a great deal of personal satisfaction, and when I accepted my first CEO role with Nymbus just months later, with a new, developing leadership team, we engaged Dean to share his valuable lessons and accelerate learning that might otherwise take years. Together, we began working with Dean through his ALP program, where we were able to extend the coaching value I gained to more people, over an extended period, for maximum impact. And the frequency and duration of our interaction in the ALP program has allowed all of us to truly integrate the learnings into our day-to-day routines.

Now, one year into my CEO role, we are seeing measurable outcomes from ALP and the teachings Dean shares in this book. Combined with the natural development of my team, Dean's principles, including his Discovery Model exercises, have brought a cohesion that's propelling us to first understand our challenges, then align and lead the entire organization to solve them. We are continuously innovating to move forward and achieving great things toward a common goal, together.

As a growth-stage company bringing innovative thinking and solutions to market—at Mach speed while doubling and tripling our employee numbers—the effectiveness of our leadership directly impacts our success. *The level of business-wide leadership alignment and collaboration we're now experiencing at Nymbus would normally take years. With Dean's guidance, it's taken us just nine months.* With the assistance of Dean's coaching, three of our first-time C-level leaders have received industry leadership awards and recognition in their respective fields. All were based on demonstrative results that contributed to our company-wide mission.

We're now on a path to achieve our goal of an IPO within our desired timeline, with a team positioned for continued growth. For our organization, the uniqueness of Dean's approach in bridging our personal, emotional and professional development and inspiring growth through this holistic lens has instilled an appetite for continued development beyond a fixed project or destination. And it's permeated throughout our organization to become part of our culture. For us, that has meant the curriculum has not only accelerated the benefits for our leadership team but has also scaled it out.

While not always at pandemic-level proportions, external influences—recession, unrest—especially the unexpected, will always exist and affect our leadership effectiveness and personal and professional missions. Dean calls these simply "disruptions." Amid disruption, we must adapt, evolve, and innovate. Building strong teams and cultures that support each other and the organizational mission is a well-placed bet on reaching optimal outcomes through whatever lies ahead. Dean puts it this way: "When you develop leaders at every level in your organization, you tap into the creative hearts and minds of your entire team."

I was fortunate enough to embark on this journey with the benefit of Dean's individual executive coaching. However, individual coaching with Dean is simply not accessible to everyone. This book, *The Missing Piece*, and the ALP program it embodies are equalizers that broaden Dean's access and influence. The powerful lessons Dean shares can have an overwhelming positive influence with your management team, and throughout your company; an influence that will convince you and your organization to adopt cultural pillars that will empower people at every level of your company.

Through personal and engaging anecdotes, practical frameworks, and a unique authentic approach, this book was a great first step toward making your desired success a reality. It captures the essence of the ALP program, and serves as a solid introduction into what is possible when you establish a culture of high-performance leaders. As Dean points out, though, the end of the book is only the beginning. I strongly encourage you to reach out and engage with Dean to continue your journey. Through Hallett Leadership's Accelerated Leadership Program, you can shift your entire organization into high performance.

Jeffery Kendall
Chairman and CEO, Nymbus
Jacksonville, Florida
2021

Bibliography

Alexis, Michael. "Team Building Statistics & Facts " *Teambuilding.com*, July 15, 2021. https://teambuilding.com/blog/team-building-statistics.

Amabile, Teresa M, and Mukti Khaire. "Creativity and the Role of the Leader." *Harvard Business Review*, August 1, 2014. https://hbr.org/2008/10/creativity-and-the-role-of-the-leader.

Cheddar Now. "How Kodak Is Reinventing Itself." YouTube video, 00:02:16. August 7, 2020. https://www.youtube.com/watch?reload=9&v=Xgolc4gcqMM

Christensen, Clayton M. *The Innovator's Dilemma*. New York, NY: Harper Business, 2011.

Collins, Jim. *Good to Great: Why Some Companies Make the Leap ... and Others Don't*. New York, NY: HarperBusiness, 2001.

Eiseley, Loren C. *The Star Thrower*. New York, NY: Harcourt Brace & Company, 1979.

Elvy, Craig. "Why the First Avatar Took so Long to Make." *ScreenRant*, August 29, 2019. https://screenrant.com/avatar-movie-development-long-reason/.

Gavin, Matt. "Authentic Leadership: What It Is & Why It's Important." *Business Insights - Blog*. Harvard Business School —Matt Online, December 10, 2019. https://online.hbs.edu/blog/post/authentic-leadership?

Gay, Wes. "Parable of the Ants.", July 25, 2018. https://wesgay.com/parable-of-the-ants/.

Goldsmith, Marshall, and Mark Reiter. *What Got You Here Won't Get You There: How Successful People Become Even More Successful*. New York, NY: Hyperion, 2007.

Goleman, Daniel. *Emotional Intelligence: Why It Can Matter More Than IQ*. 25th Anniversary Edition. New York, NY: Bantam Books, 2006.

Goleman, Daniel. *Social Intelligence*. New York, NY: Bantam Books, 2006

Gyben, Alessandra. "The Importance of ORGANIZATIONAL Alignment and How to Achieve It." *MarTech Advisor*, April 25, 2019. https://www.martechadvisor.com/articles/digital-transformation/the-importance-of-organizational-alignment-and-how-to-achieve-it/.

Harter, Jim. "Dismal Employee Engagement Is a Sign of Global Mismanagement." Gallup.com. *Gallup*, August 5, 2021. https://www.gallup.com/workplace/231668/dismal-employee-engagement-sign-global-mismanagement.aspx.

"How Organizational Alignment Creates Growth." *LSA Global*, April 21, 2021. https://lsaglobal.com/blog/organizational-alignment-creates-growth/.

LeBow, Ines. "The Importance of People in Business Success." *NABOE*, October 9, 2017. https://www.naboe.org/importance-people-business-success/.

Perry, Mark J. "Fortune 500 Firms 1955 v. 2017: Only 60 Remain, Thanks to the Creative Destruction That Fuels Economic Prosperity." *AEI.org. American Enterprise Institute*, October 20, 2017. https://www.aei.org/carpe-diem/fortune-500-firms-1955-v-2017-only-12-remain-thanks-to-the-creative-destruction-that-fuels-economic-prosperity/.

Szegedy-Maszak, Marianne. "Mysteries of the mind." *US News World Rep*. 2005 Feb 28;138(7):52-4, 57-8, 60-1. http://webhome.auburn.edu/~mitrege/ENGL2210/USNWR-mind.html

TED. "The Power of Vulnerability | Brené Brown." YouTube video, 00:20:49. January 3, 2011. https://www.youtube.com/watch?v=iCvmsMzlF7o.

"The Importance of a 'Feedback Culture' – and How You Can Build It in the Workplace." *TruQu*, November 11, 2019. https://truqu.com/en/blogs/the-importance-of-a-feedback-culture-and-how-you-can-build-it-in-the-workplace/.

www.ingramcontent.com/pod-product-compliance
Lightning Source LLC
Chambersburg PA
CBHW070755100426
42742CB00012B/2139